ABC
OF THE STEEL SQUARE
AND ITS USES

LECTOR HOUSE PUBLIC DOMAIN WORKS

ABC OF THE STEEL SQUARE AND ITS USES

FREDERICK THOMAS HODGSON

ISBN: 978-93-88396-72-1

First Published: -

LECTOR HOUSE LLP
E-MAIL: lectorpublishing@gmail.com

ABC
OF THE
STEEL SQUARE AND ITS USES

Being a condensed compilation from the copyrighted works of fred t. Hodgson, author of "the steel square and its uses," "practical carpentry" and numerous other works on building and construction.

The present compilation and new matter is made up into three divisions—a, b and c.

DIVISION A

This Division describes the various kinds of squares, their markings, their uses, and application in the solution of simple problems.

DIVISION B

This Division shows how the Square may be used for obtaining the cuts, bevels, and lengths of all sorts of rafters for roofs of every description. It also shows methods for finding Hopper and other bevels, brace cuts and lengths, and raking cornices.

DIVISION C

This shows what no other work on the Steel Square does, a number of easy solutions of Handrailing Problems, by the square. Something that has not been done or attempted in book form before. This division is made up mostly of questions and answers from practical mechanics.

COMPILED AND BROUGHT DOWN TO DATE BY
FRED T. HODGSON

WILMETTE, ILLINOIS
FREDERICK J. DRAKE & CO. PUBLISHERS

Printed in the United States of America

CONTENTS

THE STEEL SQUARE AND ITS USES.

DIVISION A.

INTRODUCTORY REMARKS.

I will not attempt in this small treatise, to give an historical account of the origin, growth and development of the square, as the subject has been treated of at length in my larger works, as I do not care to pad out these pages with matter that is not of a severely practical nature.

Suffice it to say, that while iron squares, figured on their faces in inches and feet, and smaller divisions, have been made in England and Belgium for 200 years or more, the genuine steel square, as we now know it, is a purely American product, and it has no equal, as no European manufacturer has as yet been able to turn out a square anything like as good or perfect in finish, graduation, or general get-up, as Sargent & Co., of New Haven, Conn.; Nicholls Co., Ottumwa, Iowa; and The Peck, Stow & Wilcox Co., Southington, Conn. Squares made by any one of these firms named, may be relied upon as being as near perfect as it is possible to make them in everything that pertains to accuracy, durability and general finish. The American workman should feel proud of the fact that he possesses a Steel Square of purely Home production which has no equal in the world.

There is nothing of more importance to a young man who is learning the business of house-joinery and carpentry, than that he should make himself thoroughly conversant with the capabilities of the tools he employs. It may be that, in some of the rules shown in this work, the result could be attained much readier with other aids than the square; but the progressive mechanic will not rest satisfied with one method of performing operations when others are within his reach.

In the hand of the intelligent mechanic the square becomes a simple calculating machine of the most wonderful capacity, and by it he solves problems of the kinds continually arising in mechanical work, which by the ordinary methods are more difficult to perform.

The great improvement which the arts and manufactures have attained within the last fifty years, renders it essential that every person engaged therein should use his utmost exertions to obtain a perfect knowledge of the trade he professes to follow. It is not enough, nowadays, for a person to have attained the character of a good workman; that phrase implies that quantum of excellence, which consists in working correctly and neatly, under the directions of others. The workman of to-day, to excel, must understand the principles of his trade, and be able to apply them correctly in practice. Such a one has a decided advantage over his fellow-workman; and if to his superior knowledge he possesses a steady manner, and industrious habits, his efforts cannot fail of being rewarded.

It is no sin not to know much, though it is a great one not to know all we can, and put it all to good use. Yet, how few mechanics there are who will know all they can? Men apply for employment daily who claim to be finished mechanics, and profess to be conversant with all the ins and outs of their craft, and who are noways backward in demanding the highest wages going, who, when tested, are found wanting in knowledge of the simplest formulas of their trade. They may, perhaps, be able to perform a good job of work after it is laid out for them by a more competent hand; they may have a partial knowledge of the uses and application of their tools; but, generally, their knowledge ends here. Yet some of these men have worked at this trade or that for a third of a century, and are to all appearances, satisfied with the little they learned when they were apprentices. True, mechanical knowledge was not always so easily obtained as at present, for nearly all works on the constructive arts were written by professional architects, engineers, and designers, and however unexceptionable in other respects, they were generally couched in such language, technical and mathematical, as to be perfectly unintelligible to the majority of workmen; and instead of acting as aids to the ordinary inquirer, they enveloped in mystery the simplest solutions of every-day problems, discouraging nine-tenths of workmen on the very threshold of inquiry, and causing them to abandon further efforts to master the intricacies of their respective trades.

Of late years, a number of books have been published, in which the authors and compilers have made commendable efforts to simplify matters pertaining to the arts of carpentry and joinery, and the mechanic of to-day has not the difficulties of his predecessors to contend with. The workman of old could excuse his ignorance of the higher branches of his trade, by saying that he had no means of acquiring a knowledge of them. Books were beyond his reach, and trade secrets were guarded so jealously, that only a limited few were allowed to know them, and unless he was made of better stuff than the most of his fellow-workmen, he was forced to plod on in the same groove all his days.

Not so with the mechanic of today; if he is not well up in all the minutiæ of his trade, he has but himself to blame, for although there is no royal road to knowledge, there are hundreds of open ways to obtain it; and the young mechanic who does not avail himself of one or other of these ways to enrich his mind, must lack energy, or be altogether indifferent about his trade, and may be put down as one who will never make a workman.

I have thought that it would not be out of place to preface this work on the "Steel Square," with the foregoing remarks, in the hope that they may stimulate the young mechanic, and urge him forward to conquer what at best are only imaginary difficulties. A willing heart and a clear head will most assuredly win honorable distinction in any trade, if they are only properly used. Indeed, during an experience of many years in the employment and superintendence of mechanics of every grade, from the green "wood-haggler" to the finished and accomplished workman, I have invariably discovered that the finished workman was the result of persistent study and application, and not, as is popularly supposed, a natural or spontaneous production. It is true that some men possess greater natural mechanical abilities than others, and consequently a greater aptitude in grasping the principles that underlie the constructive arts; but, as a rule, such men are not reliable; they may he expert, equal to any mechanical emergency, and quick at mastering details, but they are seldom thorough, and never reliable where long sustained efforts are required.

The mechanic who reaches a fair degree of perfection by experience, study and application is the man who rises to the surface, and whose steadiness and trustworthiness force themselves on the notice of employers and superintendents. I have said this in order to give encouragement to those young mechanics who find it up-hill work to master the intricacies of the various arts they are engaged in, for they may rest assured that in the end *work* and *application* will be sure to win; and I am certain that a thorough study of the Steel Square and its capabilities will do more than anything else to aid the young workman in mastering many of the mechanical difficulties that will confront him from time to time in his daily occupation.

It must not be supposed that the work here presented exhausts the subject. The enterprising mechanic will find opportunity for using the square in the solution of many problems that will crop up during his daily work, and the principles herein laid down will aid very much towards correct solutions. In framing roofs, bridges, trestle-work, and constructions of timber, the Steel Square is a necessity to the American carpenter; but only a few of the more intelligent workmen ever use it for other purposes than to make measurements, lay off the mortices and tenons, and square over the various joints. Now, in framing bevel work of any description, the square may be used with great advantage and profit. Posts, girts, braces, and struts of every imaginable kind may be laid out by this wonderful instrument, if the operator will only study the plans with a view of making use of his square for obtaining the various bevels, lengths and cuts required to complete the work in hand. Tapering structures—the most difficult the framer meets with—do not contain a single bevel or length that can not be found by the square when properly applied, and it is this fact I wish to impress on my readers, for it would be impossible, in this work, to give every possible application of the square to work of this kind. I have, therefore, only given such examples as will enable any one to apply some one of them to any work in hand.

In the foregoing sketch I have given a few hints as to the kind of square to purchase when it is necessary to buy; in many cases, however, this book will find its way into the hands of mechanics and others, who will have old and favorite squares in their chests or workshops, and who will not care to dispose of a "well-tried friend" for the purpose of filling its place with another, simply because I have recommended it. To these workmen I would say that I do not advise a change, provided the old square is true, and the inches and sub-divisions are properly and accurately defined. I wish it distinctly understood that old squares, if true, and marked with inches and sub-divisions of inches, will perform nearly every solution presented in this book.

The lines and figures formed on the squares of different make, sometimes vary, both as to their position on the square, and their mode of application, but a thorough understanding of the application of the scales and lines shown on any first-class tool, will enable the student to comprehend the use of the lines and figures exhibited on other first-class squares.

To insure good results, it is necessary to be careful in the selection of the tool. The blade of the square should be 24 inches long, and two inches wide, and the tongue from 14 to 18 inches long and 1½ inches wide. The tongue should be exactly at right angles with the blade, or in other words the "square" should be perfectly square.

To test this question, get a board, about 12 or 14 inches wide, and four feet long, dress it on one side, and true up one edge as near straight as it is possible to make it. Lay the board on the bench, with the dressed side up, and the trued edge towards you, then apply the square, with the blade to the left, and mark across the prepared board with a penknife blade, pressing close against the edge of the tongue; this process done to your satisfaction, reverse the square, and move it until the tongue is close up to the knife mark; if you find that the edge of the tongue and mark coincide, it is proof that the tool is correct enough for your purposes. Later on, I will show by diagram how this test is performed.

This, of course, relates to the outside edge of the blade, and the outside edge of the tongue. If these edges should not be straight, or should not prove perfectly true, they should be filed or ground until they are straight and true. The outside edge of the blade should also be "trued" up and made exactly parallel with the inside edge, if such is required. The same process should be gone through on the tongue. As a rule, squares made by firms of repute are perfect, and require no adjusting; nevertheless, it is well to make a critical examination before purchasing.

The next thing to be considered is the use of the figures, lines, and scales, as exhibited on the square. It is supposed that the ordinary divisions and sub-divisions of the inch, into halves, quarters, eighths, and sixteenths are understood by the student; and that he also understands how to use that part of the square that is subdivided into twelfths of an inch. This being conceded, we now proceed to describe the various rules as shown on all good squares; but before proceeding further, it may not be out of place to state, that on the squares recommended in this book, one edge is subdivided into thirty-seconds of an inch.

This fine sub-division will be found very useful, particularly so when used as a scale to measure drawings made in half, one-quarter, one-eighth or one-sixteenth of an inch to the foot.

PRACTICAL USES OF THE STEEL SQUARE

We now take up a square void of any attachments, and one which has become quite popular in the west and the middle southern states. I refer to the "Nicholls Square," a representation of one side of which is shown at Fig. 1. This square is a new one on the market, and presents some advantages over many now being sold. The manufacturers direct special attention to the fact that the board measure has been replaced by a simple rule for framing, and that there is to be found the lengths and figures giving the cuts for an entire roof, also the cuts for cornice of the same. The tongue on the square is 1¾ inches wide, thus making it convenient for spacing, as much of the dimension lumber is 1¾ inches thick. The general directions for using this square—a copy of which is given to every purchaser of a square—are presented herewith, so that the reader will be able himself to judge of the merits of the tool. These squares are numbered or graded according to the graduation marks and quality of finish.

Fig. 1.

"The face of a square is the side on which we stamp our name. The reverse is the back. The longer arm is the body, the other is the tongue.

Framing Rule.—The first line of figures gives the length of common rafters for one foot run. The second line of figures gives the length of hip or valley rafters for one foot run.

The third line of figures gives the length of first jack rafter and the difference in the length of the others spaced 16 inches on centers.

The fourth line of figures gives the length of first jack rafters and the difference in the length of the others spaced 2 feet on centers.

The fifth line of figures gives the side cut of jack rafters against hip or valley rafters.

The sixth line of figures gives the side cut of hip or valley rafter against ridge board or deck.

The seventh line of figures gives the cuts of sheathing and shingles in valley or hip, for example:

If your roof is raised 8 inches to the foot, or, as it is called, third pitch, under 8 on the first line are the figures 14.42. This is the length of common rafters for one foot run. If the building is 16 feet wide half the width of building would be the run of common rafter. In this case it would be 8; multiply 14.42 by 8, you have 115.36 inches, or 9 feet 7⅜ inches.

To obtain the bottom and top cuts of common rafter use the figures 12 on body and 8 on tongue; 12 side gives bottom cut, 8 side gives top cut; the same figures give bottom and top cuts for jack.

On the second line under 8 are the figures 18.78; multiply these figures by 8, which is the run of the common rafter. This gives 150.24, or 12 feet 6¼ inches. This is the correct length of hip or valley rafter. To obtain the bottom and top cuts for hip or valley rafters, use the figures 17 on body and 8 on tongue; 17 side gives bottom cut, 8 side gives top cut.

This is all the figuring necessary to be done. The reason for giving the lengths for one foot of common and hip or valley rafters is that it will work in all cases regardless of width of buildings.

On the third line under 8 are the figures 19¼ inches. This is the length of first jack rafter, also the difference in the length of the others spaced 16 inches on centers. For example, the first jack being 19¼ inches, the second jack would be 3 feet 2½ inches; make each one 19¼ inches longer than the other.

On the fourth line under 8 are the figures 2 feet 4⅞ inches. This is the length of the first jack rafter, and the difference in the length of the others spaced 2 feet centers.

On the fifth line under 8 are the figures 10 and 12. By placing square on stock to be cut at these figures 10 on body, 12 on tongue, and marking on 12 side this gives side cut of jacks against hip or valley rafter.

On the sixth line under 8 are the figures 9 and 10. By placing square on stock to be cut at these figures, 9 on body and 10 on tongue, and marking on the 10 side, this gives side cut of hip or valley rafter against ridge board or deck.

On the seventh line under 8 are figures 12 and 10. By placing square on stock to be cut at these figures 12 on body, 10 on tongue, and marking on the 10 side this gives the cut of sheathing and shingles in valley or hip.

Remarks.—To obtain the lengths and cuts be careful to use the figures under whatever figure your roof raises to the foot. If your roof raises 12 inches to the foot, or half pitch, look under 12, and so on in all cases. In cutting jack rafters allow for half the thickness of hip or valley rafters as lengths given on square are to center lines.

Note.—The figures on the square, giving side cuts of jacks, will also give the correct miter cuts for moulding in the valley at the junction of two gables, also miter cuts for gable mouldings where it intersects with level mouldings at the end of building.

The figures giving cuts of sheathing in valley or hip also give cuts for mitering level planceer with gable planceer, also the miter cuts where two gable planceers intersect, also the cut for planceer on gable end.

To obtain the bottom and top cuts of hip or valley rafter use the figure 17 on body, and whatever figure your roof raises to the foot on tongue. This will give you the correct cuts in all cases.

To obtain the bottom and top cuts of common rafters and jack rafters use the figure 12 on body, and whatever figure your roof raises to the foot on tongue. This gives correct cuts in all cases. Always remember that the cut comes on the tongue, or last named figure. It is so arranged in all cases.

Octagon, "Eight-square" Scale.—This scale is along the middle of the face of the tongue, and is used for laying off lines to cut an "eight square" or octagon stick of timber from a square.

Suppose the figures A, B, C, D, Fig. 2, is the butt of a square stick of timber 6×6 inches. Through the center draw the lines AB and CD parallel with the sides and at right angles to each other.

With the dividers take us many spaces (6) from the scale as there are inches in the width of the stick, and lay off this space on either side of the point A as Aa and Ab; lay off in the same way the space from the point B as Bd and Be; also Cf and Cg and Db and De. Then draw the lines ab, cd, cf and gh. Cut off the solid angle E, also F, G and H; there is left an octagon, or "eight square" stick. This is nearly exact.

Brace Measure.—This is along the center of the back of the "tongue," and gives the length of the common brace.

18 13 25.45 in the scale means that if the run is 18 inches on the post and the same on the beam, then the brace will be 25 45-100 inches.

If the run is 21 inches on both beam and post, then the brace will be 29 70-100 inches.

Care of Square.—Never use emery or sand paper on nickel or black finished squares. When through using put on a few drops of oil. Do not put your square away with finger marks on it; nothing rusts it so quickly as perspiration."

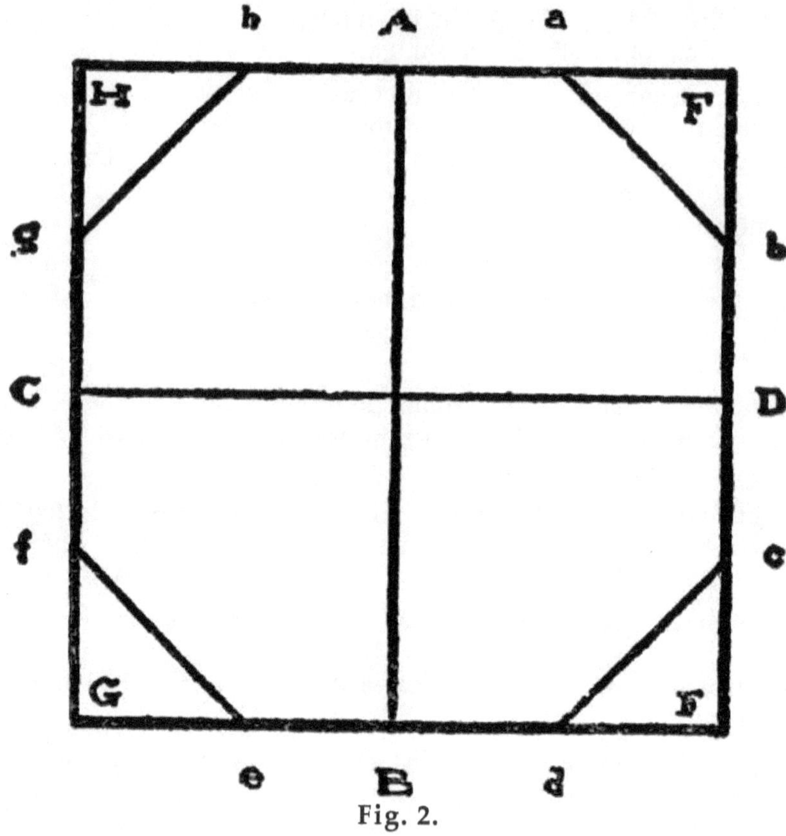

Fig. 2.

It will be seen that these squares adapt themselves to other work as well as to framing, a quality very few of the combination squares possess, and while combination squares have their special uses and should be in the tool chest of every expert workman, the square pure and simple, like this of Nicholls or similar ones, should never be absent from the "kit" of the ordinary workman, for with it, if he thoroughly understands it, he can accomplish all that is possible even with a combination square. If he is not "posted" the workman should procure some one or more of the many devices or helps for getting bevels, angles, lengths and cuts, for rafters, braces, hips and jacks as advertised by Riesmann, Woods, and others.

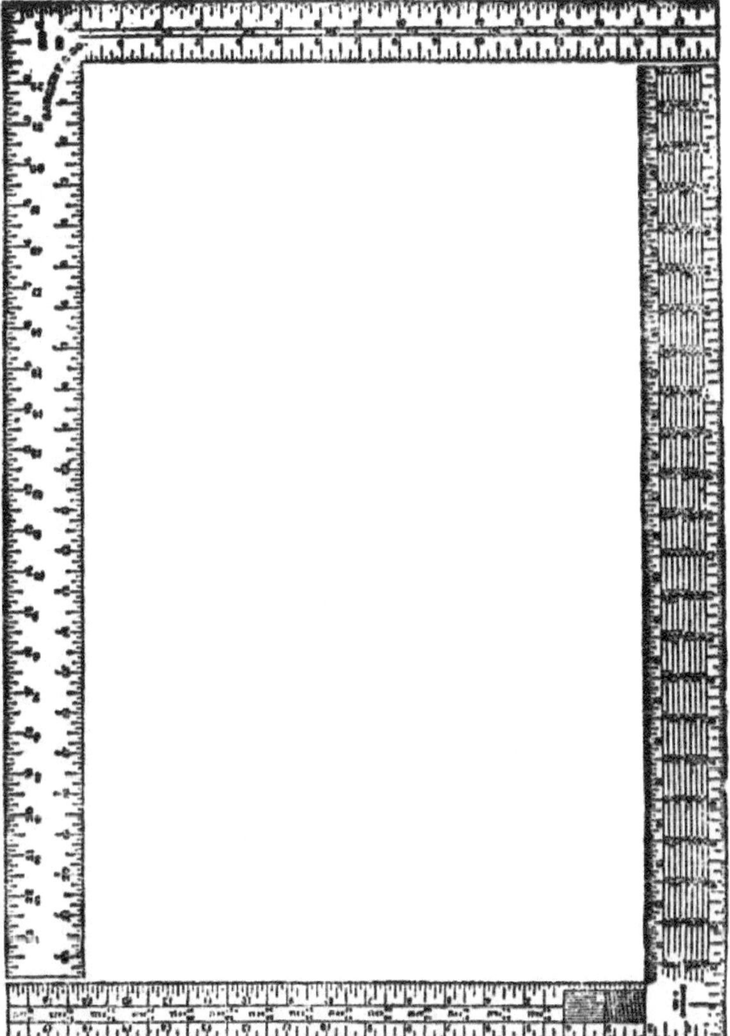

Fig. 3.

With these aids and a good true and honest steel square the workman can accomplish almost all that can be done with this tool, or all that he will be called upon to execute by aid of the square.

These squares are furnished by the manufacturers either in polished steel, nickel plate or oxidized copper. The latter style is quite popular with some workmen, because of its not getting so hot when exposed to the rays of the sun.

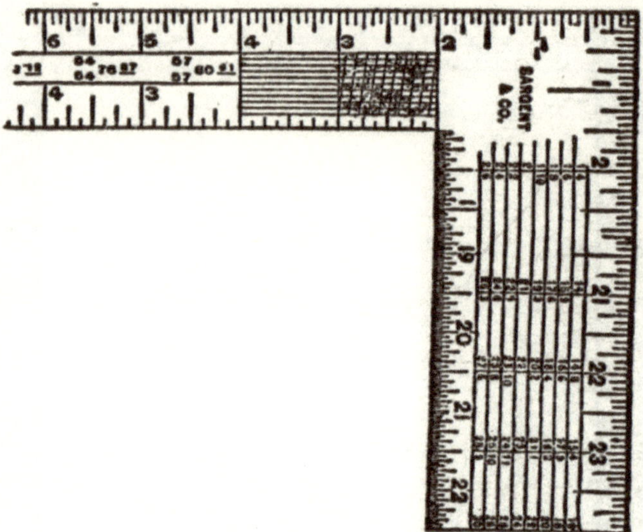

Fig. 4.

The two sides of the square, shown at Fig. 3, represent the carpenters' popular square, No. 100. This square has been a special favorite with workmen for nearly thirty years, and is still looked upon by many as being the *ne plus ultra* of steel squares. I show both sides of the square in order to enable the workman to see, before he buys, the kind of tool he will get. Like the Nicholls square, this may be obtained in polished steel, nickel plated, or oxidized copper as the purchaser may desire.

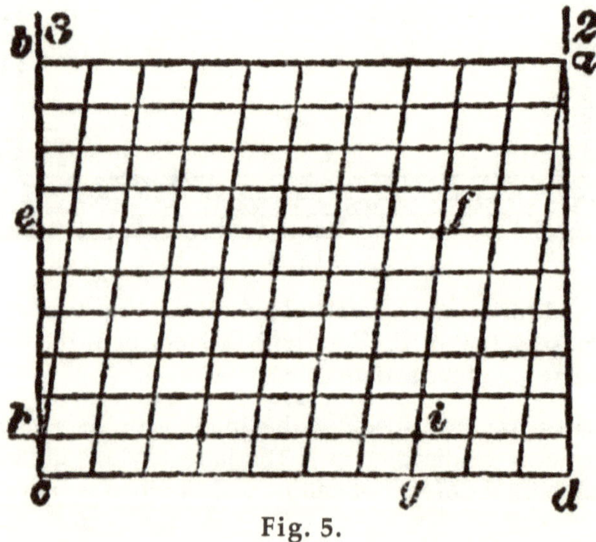

Fig. 5.

I show the complete square, reduced to page size. Sometimes this square is catalogued by dealers as No. 1000, practically, however, it is the same square as the No. 100. If we examine this square we will find on the tongue near its junction with the blade a series of lines and cross lines (see Fig. 4), making a figure known as the "diagonal scale." This scale is drawn to a larger size at Fig. 5 and is shown alone and is used for taking off the hundredths of an inch. The line *ab* is here an inch long, and is divided into ten equal parts; the line *cd* being also divided into ten equal parts, and diagonal lines are then drawn connecting the points as shown in the diagram. Suppose we wish to take off 76-100 of an inch, we proceed as follows: Count off seven spaces from *c, e, g,* which equals 70-100 of an inch; then count up the diagonal line until the sixth horizontal line, *e,* is reached, when *e f* will equal the required distance of 76-100 of an inch, which is a trifle over ¾ of an inch.

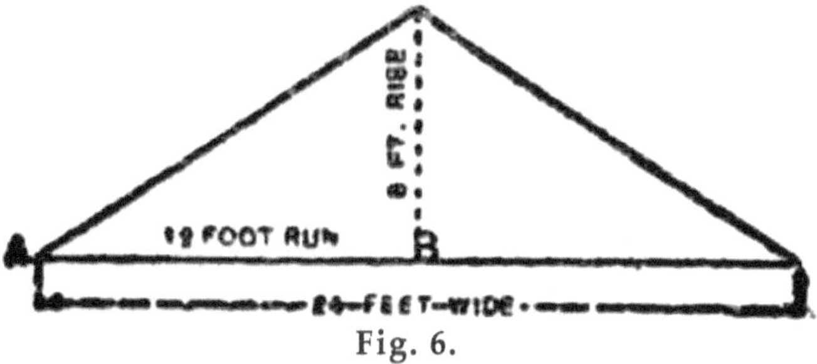

Fig. 6.

Quoting from the table of directions given in Sargent's circular describing this square, we have, for rafter cuts, the following explanation: "This run of a rafter set up in place is the horizontal measure from the extreme end of the foot to a plumb-line from the ridge end—from A to B, Fig. 6.

Fig. 7.

"The rise is the distance from the top of the ridge end of the rafter to the level of the foot. From C to D, Fig. 7.

"The pitch is the proportion that the rise bears to the whole width of the building. The illustration, Fig. 8, shows one-third pitch; the rise of 8 foot being one-third of the width of the building.

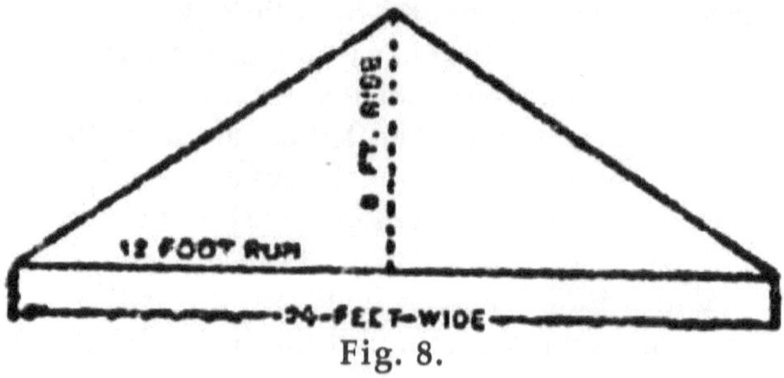

Fig. 8.

"The cuts or angles of a rafter are obtained by applying the square so that the 12-inch mark on the body and the mark on the tongue that represent the rise shall both be at the edge of the rafter. The illustration, Fig. 9, shows 8 foot rise, the line A the cut for the ridge end of the rafter and B the cut for foot end."

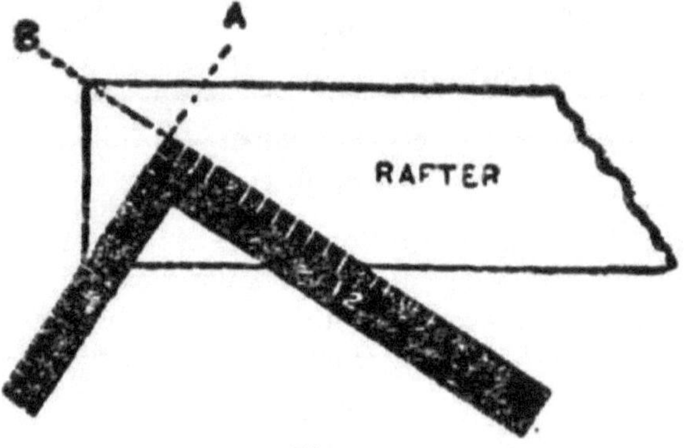

Fig. 9.

The portion of square shown at Fig. 10 exhibits the tool having on its face a table of the run, rise and pitch of rafters, being specially figured for this purpose, and shows the measure of the rafter for any one of seven pitches of roof based upon the length of the horizontal measurement of the building from the center to the outside.

The following table, which was prepared especially for this square, shows the manner of working the square:

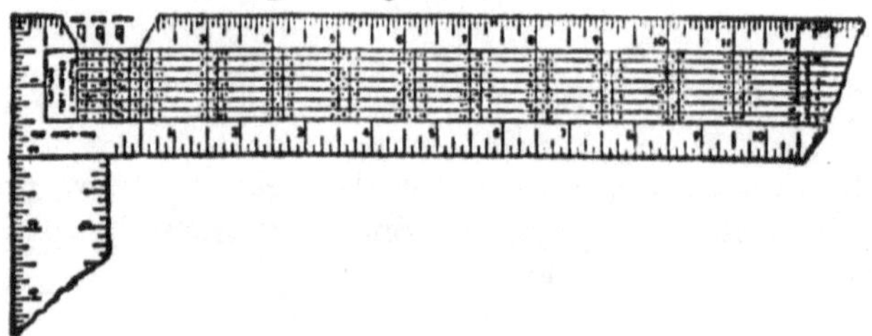

Fig. 10.

RAFTER TABLE DIRECTIONS.

The rafter table and the outside edge of the back of the square, both on body and tongue, are in twelfths. The inch marks may represent inches or feet, and the twelfth marks may represent twelfths of an inch or twelfths of a foot (that is, inches) as a scale. The rafter table is used in connection with the marks and figures on the outside edge of the square.

At the left end of the table are figures representing the *run*, the *rise* and the *pitch*.

In the first column the figures are all 12, which may be used as 12 inches or 12 feet, and they represent a *run* of 12.

The second column of figures is to represent various *rises*.

The third column of figures in fractions represents the various *pitches*.

These three columns of figures show that a rafter with a run of 12 and a rise of 4 has 1-6 pitch, with a run of 12 and a rise of 6 has 1-4 pitch, with a run of 12 and a rise of 8 has 1-3 pitch, and so on to the bottom of the figures.

To Find the Length of a Rafter.—For a roof with 1-6 pitch (or the rise 1-6 the width of the building) and having a run of 12 feet, follow in the rafter table the upper 1-6 pitch ruling, find under the graduation figure 12 the rafter length required, which is 12 7 10, or 12 feet and 7 10-12 inches.

For ½ pitch (or the rise ½ the width of the building) and run 12 feet, the rafter length is 16 11 8, or 16 feet 11 8-12 inches.

If the run is 25 feet, add the rafter length for run of 23 feet to the rafter length for run of 2 feet.

When the run is in inches, then in the rafter table read inches and twelfths instead of feet and inches. For instance:

If with ½ pitch the run is 12 feet 4 inches, add the rafter length of 12 feet to that of 4 inches, as follows:

For run of 12 feet the rafter length is   16 feet 11 8-12 inches. For run of 4 inches the rafter length is   5 8-12 inches. Total   17 feet 5 4-12 inches.

The brace measure on these squares is along the center of the back of the tongue, and gives the length of the common braces as shown in Fig. 11. Examples are shown in the blade as at the point marked 24 30, which means 24 inches on the post and 18 inches on the beam or girt, which make the brace 30 inches long from point to point according to the rule given. An application of this rule is shown at Fig. 12, where 36 inches are laid off on both post and beam, which gives the length of the brace from point to point 50.91 inches, or very nearly 4 feet 3 inches. Other dimensions are shown in the square. There is also a scale of one-hundredths, or one inch divided into 100 equal parts.

The octagon scale on this square runs along the middle of the face of the tongue, and is used for laying off lines to cut an "eight square" or octagon stick of timber from a square one.

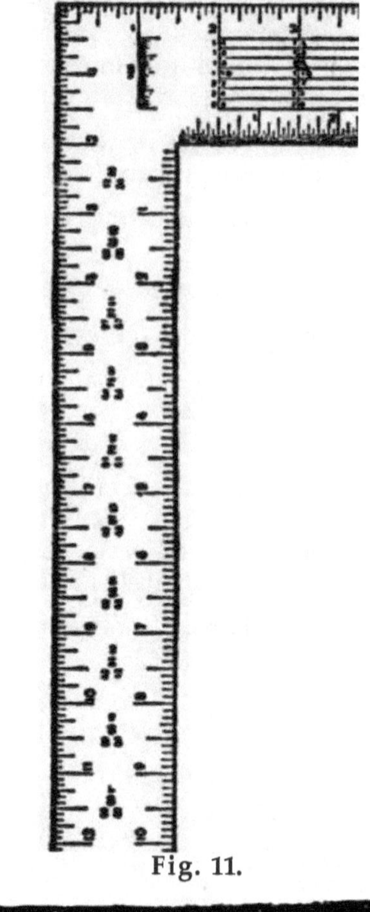

Fig. 11.

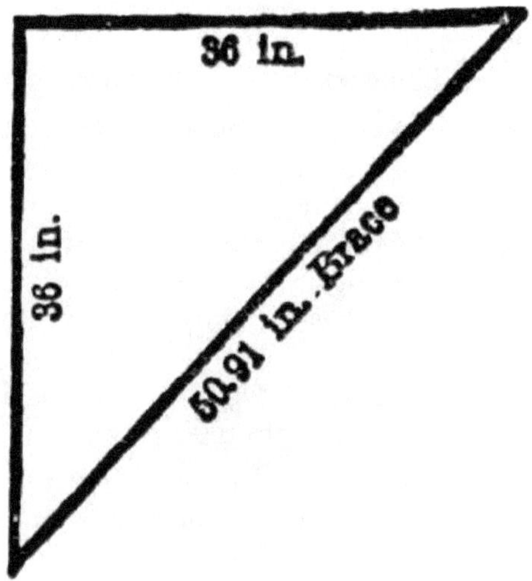

Fig. 12.

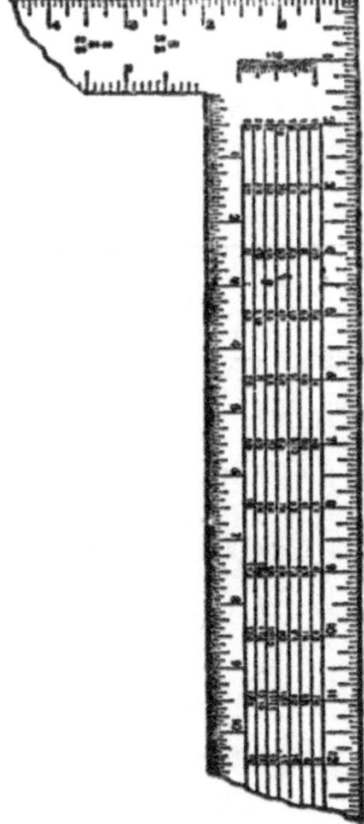

Fig. 13.

Suppose the figure ABCD (see Fig. 2) is the butt of a square stick of timber 6x6 inches. Through the center draw the lines AB and CD parallel with the sides and at right angles to each other. With a pair of compasses take as many spaces (6) from the scale as there are inches in the width of the stick, and lay off this space on either side of the point A, as Aa and Ab; lay off in the same way the same space from the point B as Bd, Be; also Cf, Cg and Db, Dc. Then draw lines ab, cd, ef and gh. Cut off the solid angle E, also F, G and H. This will leave an octagon, or eight-sided stick, which will be found nearly exact on all sides.

The board measure, known as the "Essex Board Measure," Fig. 13, is made use of in figuring these squares, and is used as follows: Figures 12 and 17 in the graduation marks on the outer edge represent a one-inch board 12 inches wide, which is the starting point for all calculations. The smaller figures under the 12 represent the length.

A board 12 inches wide and 8 feet long measures 8 square feet, and so on down the table. Therefore, to get the square feet of a board 8 feet long and 6 inches wide, find the figure 8 in the scale under the 12- inch graduation mark and pass the pencil along to the left on the same line to a point below the graduation mark 6 (representing the width of the board), and you stop on the scale at 4, which is 4 feet, the board measure required. If the board is the same length and 10 inches wide, look under the graduation mark 10 on a line with the figure 8 before mentioned, and you will find 6 8-12 feet board measure; if 18 inches wide then to the right under the graduation mark 18 and 12 feet is found to be the board measure. If 13 feet long and 7 inches wide, find 13 in the scale under the 12-inch graduation and on the same line under the 7-inch graduation will be found 7 7-12 feet board measure. If the board is half this length, take half of this result; if double this length, then double this result. For stuff 2 inches thick double the figure.

In this way the scale covers all lengths of boards, the most common from 8 feet to 15 feet being given.

This company also manufactures a square that is "blued," or apparently oxidized, with all the figures on it enameled in white. This is really a handsome tool, and the white figures on a dark blue ground enable the operator to see what figures he is looking for without waste of time and straining of eyesight.

Fig. 14.

The bridge builders' steel square, which is illustrated in Fig. 14, is also made by this company. This square has a blade three inches wide, which is made with a slot down the center one inch wide. The tongue is the same as in the No. 100 square, but has no figures for brace or octagon rules. It is not so handy for general purposes as the regular square, but for special purposes in bridge building, or for laying out very heavy timber structures it has special advantages, as 3-inch shoulders and 3-inch tenons and mortises can be readily laid out with it. Another square, shown in Fig. 15, known as the "machinists' square," is made by this company. It has a blade 6 inches and a tongue 4 inches long, and is very finely finished. This square is found very useful for pattern makers, piano and organ builders, and where other especially close work is required. A number of other squares are made by this firm, but as they are not intended for woodworkers' use, I will not describe them here.

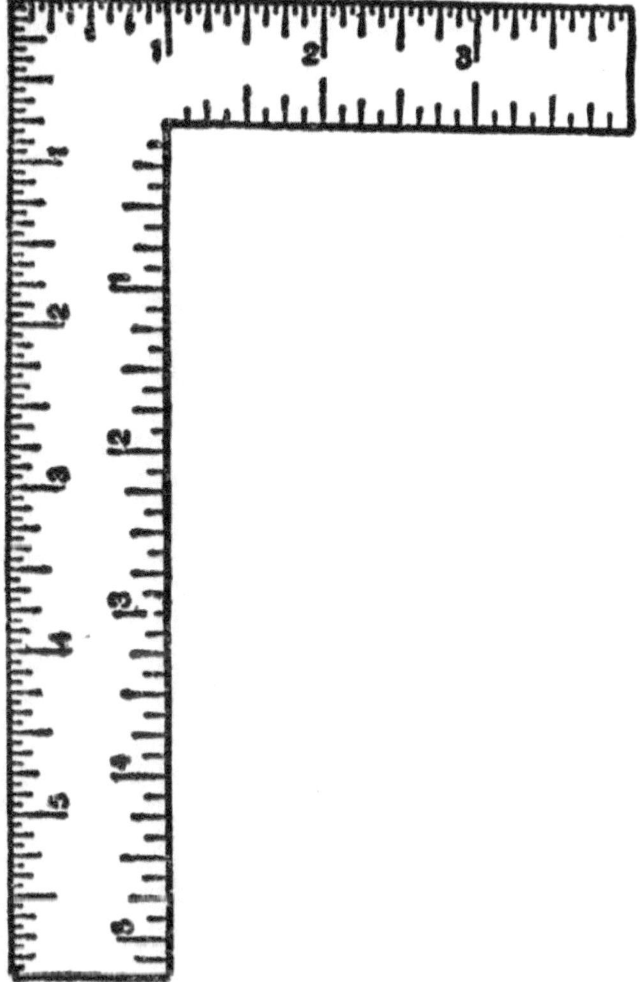

Fig. 15.

I would not complete this description of Sargent's make of squares if I failed to make mention of their "bench square." I give this name to it because of its fitness for bench purposes. The square referred to has a blade 12 inches long and 1½ inches wide, and a tongue 9 inches long and 1 inch wide. The figuring on it is divided into inches, half inches, quarter inches, eighths and sixteenths of an inch. This is a very handy square for bench and jobbing purposes, and can be used in many places where the larger tool is unavailable, and may on emergency be employed for laying out rafters, braces and similar work. A square that was quite popular some sixteen or eighteen years ago known as "The Crenalated Square," an illustration of which is shown in Fig. 16, is still preferred by many workmen. The peculiarity of this square is that the inner edge of the tongue is notched or crenalated, as shown in the illustration, the notches being intended as "gauge-points," where a sharpened pencil may be inserted, then the square may be drawn along the timber or board, with the blade held snug against the edge, as shown, and mortises or tenons can be laid out at will.

Besides being crenalated, these squares have all the advantages of other squares, and are well made and pleasant to handle. They are made by the manufacturers, The Peck, Stowe & Wilcox Co., of Southington, Conn., in polished steel, copper plated, blued, with enameled white figures, and in nickel plate.

Fig. 16.

It is the simplest of tools, and may be described as the mechanical embodiment of a right angle. It must necessarily have some breadth in order to give the tool necessary stability, and, therefore, as the embodiment of a right angle it is of a form to give us both the exterior and interior shape. The blade of the square is made a little wider than the tongue, more for convenience, I think, than for any other reason, for I have seen squares somewhat old, to be sure, and made long before the tools which are now in most common use were sent out from the factory, of which the blade and tongue were approximately of the same width.

The blade of the square, as commonly constructed, is 2 feet, or 24 inches long, and the tongue somewhat less. I have seen squares of which the tongue and blade were of equal lengths, and also those, the blade of which were considerably longer than those of the square of present make, and still others of which the tongues were considerably shorter than is now the rule. But this is long ago. The most commonly accepted dimensions for a carpenter's square at the present time are, blade 24 inches long, tongue 18 inches long, blade 2 inches wide and tongue 1½ inches wide. This gives for inside measurements blade, 22½ inches and tongue 16 inches.

I have described the square as the embodiment of a right angle. If the square is not a right angle, or to use common terms, if the tool is "out of square," that is, if it is in the least inaccurate, its usefulness is destroyed. When the square is inaccurate instead of solving intricate geometrical problems correctly it becomes a snare and a delusion, leading to false results and misfits in general. It is somewhat remarkable how few workmen test their squares. I am disposed to believe from long experience that comparatively few mechanics who buy steel squares are cognizant of the possible defects that the tool may have and of the tests which may be applied for the purpose of demonstrating its accuracy. Before proceeding further, therefore, in the discussion of the use of this instrument let us give brief attention to some of the simple methods that may be employed for determining the accuracy of the tool. By way of making practical application of these tests I suggest that at the next dinner hour the reader borrow from his fellow carpenters as many squares as may be convenient, and apply to them more or less of the tests which follow, merely for the purpose of practice, and at the same time to show to what extent the squares in use are correct.

Fig. 17 shows a very common method of testing the exterior angle of a steel square. Two squares are placed against each other and a straight-edge, or against the blade of a third square. If the edges of the squares exactly coincide throughout the squares may be considered correct.

Fig. 17.

Suppose, however, that there is a discrepancy shown by this test, and that as the two squares are placed in the general position, shown in the illustration, they part at the heel, while touching at the ends of the blades, or touching at the heel that they part at the ends of the blades. This evidently shows that one of the squares is inaccurate, or possibly that both are inaccurate. How is the inaccuracy to be located? The two squares may be placed face to face, with the blades upward from an even surface, say the face of the third square or the jointed edge of a board, and so held that their heels, for example, shall coincide. Then glance at the edges of the blades. If they exactly coincide it would indicate that the error is evenly divided between the two squares, a very improbable occurrence. Compare the two squares in the reverse position, that is, with the tongues extending upward. Then apply the test shown in Fig. 18, and finally that shown in Fig. 19.

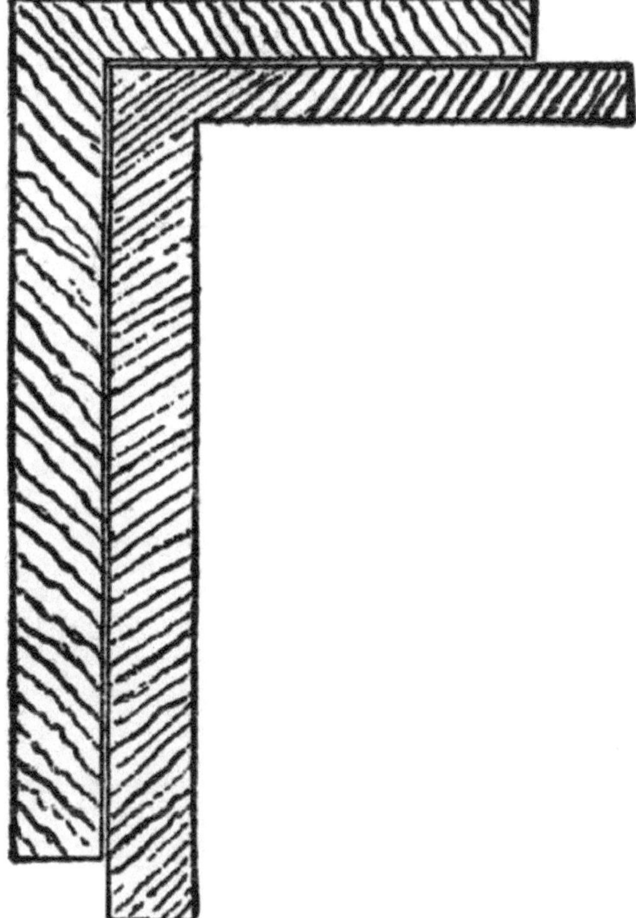

Fig. 18.

By trying the squares one inside of the other, as shown in Fig. 18, the exterior angle is compared with the interior angle. If the edges throughout fit together tightly, first using one square inside and then the other, it is lmost conclusive evidence that both the squares are accurate.

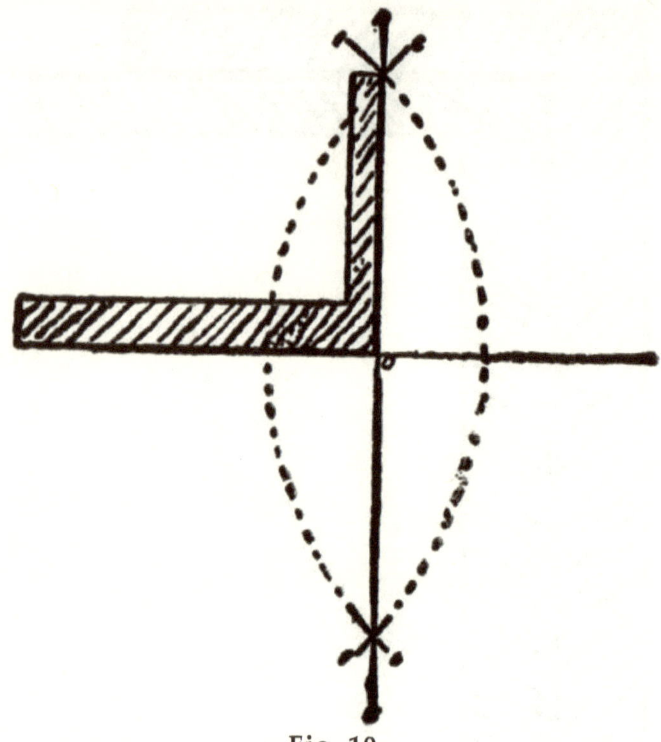

Fig. 19.

By tests of the kinds just described among several squares, the mechanic will soon perceive from the several ascertained results that one or the other of the several squares that he is handling is more accurate than all the others, if not absolutely accurate. There still remains the need of a test, however, to prove the absolute accuracy of the particular square which he believes to be about right. On a drafting table, or a smooth board, let him next perform the following experiment, which is one of the several that might be mentioned in this connection: Draw a straight line, AB, say three feet in length, as shown in Fig. 19. This may be done by a straight-edge. Use a hard pencil sharpened to a chisel point. With the compasses, using A and B as centers, and with a radius longer than one-half of AB strike the arcs CD and EF. Then with the straight-edge draw a straight line, GH, through the intersection of the arcs. If the work is accurately done the resulting angles AOH, HOB, BOG, and GOA will be right angles. Lay the square to be tested onto one of these angles, as shown in the illustration, and with a chisel-pointed pencil scribe along the blade and along the tongue. If the lines thus drawn exactly coincide with those first drawn it is satisfactory proof that the square is accurate, and in the same way the square may be placed against one or the other of these right angles in a way to test its interior angle.

The method shown in Fig. 19 anticipates the use of another tool besides the square in making the test. A right angle, however, may be drawn for the purpose described by a method which uses only the square, and which does not require the services of any other tool, or what is the same thing, consider the tool itself to be the figure drawn, and then measure for the purpose of determining the accuracy of the figure.

Various writers have discussed the properties of the right-angled triangle, but we all know that a square erected on a hypothenuse of a right-angled triangle is equal to the sum of the squares erected on the base and perpendicular. This is a well-known mathematical truth, and it may be applied in the tests we are making. Those carpenters who have had occasion to lay out the foundations of houses are well acquainted with the old rule frequently known as "the 6, 8 and 10," which depends upon the relationship of the squares of the perpendicular and the base to the square of the hypothenuse. Thus the square of 6 is 36, the square of 8 is 64. The sum of 36 and 64 is 100. And the square of 10 is 100. Now let us make application of this rule to test the steel square.

For the sake of accuracy we want to take figures which are as large as possible, so as to reduce the possible error in measurement to the smallest possible dimensions. Let us take for dimensions, 9, 12 and 15 inches. That these will serve is easily demonstrated. The square of 9 is 81. The square of 12 is 144. The sum of these squares is 225, and the square of 15 is 225. Therefore, if the tool that we are testing shows a dimension of exactly 15 inches measured from 9 on the outside of the tongue to 12 on the outside of the blade, as shown in Fig. 20, it will be proof that the square is correct.

It may be somewhat difficult to make a measurement of this kind on the instrument itself, with sufficient accuracy to be beyond dispute. I suggest, therefore, that the square be laid flat upon an even surface, like a drawing table, and that with a chisel-pointed pencil lines be scribed along the tongue and along the blade. Mark accurately the distance of 9 inches from the heel up the tongue, and 12 inches from the heel along the blade. Then measure diagonally and see if the distance is exactly 15 inches.

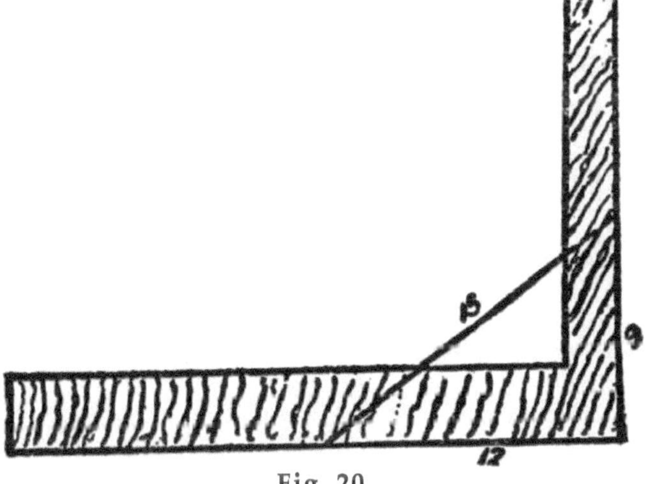

Fig. 20.

In what has preceded there has been a suggestion that the error due to lack of precision in measurement is diminished if the figures are increased in size. If the size of the drafting table permits, therefore, extend the line drawn along the tongue of the square to 3 feet. Extend that drawn along the blade to 4 feet. In doing this care must be taken that the lines thus extended are fair to the tool under examination, for if they are not drawn in a way to strictly coincide with the edges of the square then the test is of no avail. Then measure from the ends of these lines, that is, from a point 3 feet from the heel up the tongue to a point 4 feet from the heel along the blade. If this diagonal distance is exactly 5 feet it will show that the angle represented by the heel of the square, as I have described it, is a right angle, and that, therefore, the test is accurate.

Now let us next examine a little more carefully the relationship of the square to frequently required lines. It is a common thing among carpenters to use 12 of the blade and 12 of the tongue for a right angle or square miter. Why are these figures employed, or to put the question otherwise, how is it determined that 12 and 12 are the proper figures? Perhaps the question can be made still clearer by another illustration. It is common to say that 12 of the blade and 5 of the tongue is correct for the octagon miter. How is this determined? In Fig. 21 there is shown a quarter circle, XG, described from the center C. Along the horizontal line, AB, the blade of the square is laid with 12 of the blade against the center C, from which the quadrant was struck. Now if we divide this quadrant into halves, thus establishing the point E, and if from E we draw a line to the center C, which is 12 of the blade, it will be found that it cuts also 12 of the tongue. If we complete the figure by erecting a perpendicular line from the point X, and intersecting it with a horizontal line from G, thus establishing the point O, it becomes very evident that CE is the miter line of a square.

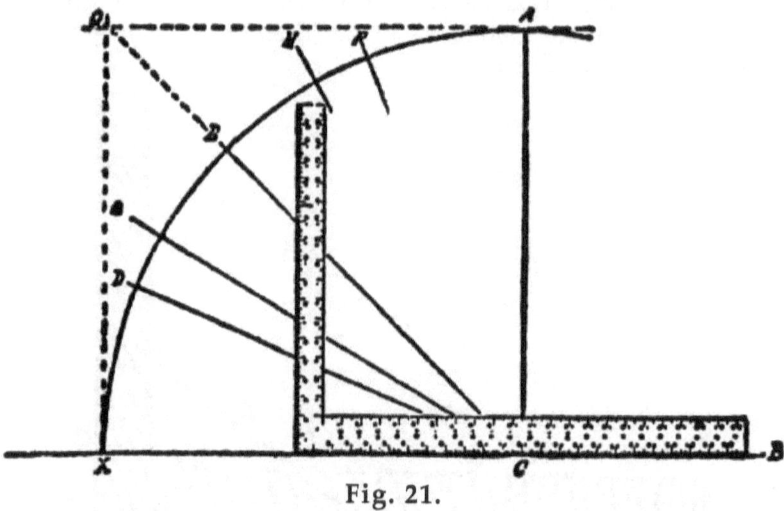

Fig. 21.

If we bisect XE, thus establishing the point D, and by the conditions existing setting off in the quadrant a space equal to one-quarter of its extent, and if from D we draw a line to the center, C, corresponding, as already mentioned, with 12 on the blade, we shall find that this line (DC) cuts the tongue on the point 5 (very nearly, the exact figures being 4 31-32 inches). The line DC, as above explained, bisects the eighth of a circle. In other words, it is the line of an octagon miter, and therefore, we say that for an octagon miter we take 12 on the blade and 5 on the tongue.

By dividing the quadrant into three equal parts, as shown by XG, GH and HG, we obtain by drawing GC the line corresponding to the hexagon miter. This, it will be observed, cuts the tongue of the square at 7 (very nearly, the exact figures being 6 15-16 inches), and, therefore, we say for hexagon miters we take 12 of the blade and 7 of the tongue.

The question sometimes arises, can the square be employed to describe a circle? While the square may be used for describing a circle of any diameter, providing the capacity of the square is not exceeded, still those who attempt to perform the work will very likely conclude before they are through that other means are more satisfactory for regular use. The way to proceed is indicated in Fig. 22. Let it be required to describe a circle, the diameter of which is equal to ED. Drive pins or nails at these points and place the square as shown in the sketch. Place a pencil in the interior angle of the square, as shown at F. Then gradually shift the square so that the pencil will move in the direction of D, always being careful to keep the inside of the blade and inside of the tongue in contact with the pins or nails, ED. After having described the arc from F to D reverse the direction describing the arc from F to E. Then turn the square over and by similar means complete the other half of the circle.

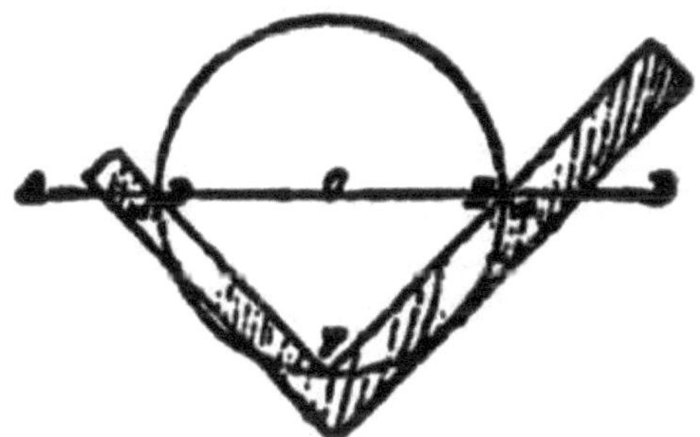

Fig. 22.

THE STEEL SQUARE AND ITS USES.

DIVISION B.

INTRODUCTORY.

Having dealt with the more simple matters that can be dealt with by aid of the Steel Square, we now take up some of the more difficult problems that can be solved by aid of this useful tool.

Among the problems and solutions offered, are those of laying out braces, having regular or irregular runs, rafters, and roofing generally, ascertaining the length of hips, their bevels, cuts, pitches and angles, jacks, cripples, ridges, purlins, collar beams, and much other matter pertaining to hip or cottage roofs.

Gables, or saddle roofs are dealt with, also mansard roofs, taper framing, odd bevels, splays and other similar work.

I introduce in this division a few remarks regarding the fence made use of when laying out rafters, stairs or other bevelled work. The department also shows how to lay-out stair strings by aid of the square, and many other things that will be found useful to the general workman.

DOUBLE SLOTTED FENCE.

Fig. 23:

Fig. 24.

A very good fence for the square may readily be made from a stick of hardwood (Fig. 23) about two inches wide, one and a half inches thick and two and a half feet long. A saw kerf, into which the square will slide, is cut from both ends leaving about 8 inches of solid wood near the middle. The tool is clamped to the square by means of screws at convenient points as shown. Another style of fence, which is made of a piece of hardwood, has a single slot only as shown in Fig. 24. The square is slipped in and fastened in place by screws similar to the first. An application of the fence and square combined is shown at Fig. 25, where the combination is used as a pitch-board for laying out stair strings. In this example the blade is set off at 10 inches, which makes the tread, and the tongue shows the riser, which is set off at 7 inches. The dotted line, *ce*, shows the edge of the plank from which the string is cut, and *h* shows the fence, *a* shows the bottom tread and riser. In this example the riser shows the same height as the riser above it, namely, 7 inches. This is wrong, as the first riser should always be cut the *thickness of the tread less* than those above it, as shown by the dotted lines on the bottom of the string, then when the tread is in place it will be the same height from the top of the floor to the top of the first tread, that the top of first tread is to top of second one and so on.

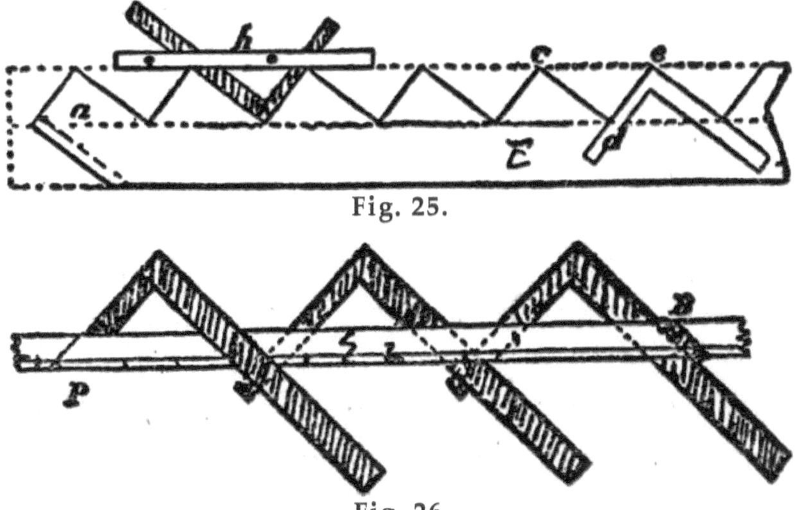

Fig. 25.

Fig. 26.

Suppose we wish to lay out a rafter having eight inches rise and twelve inches run. Set the fence at the 8″ mark on the blade, Fig. 26, and at the 12″ mark on the tongue, clamping it to the square with 1¼″ screws. Applying the square and fence at the upper end of the rafter we get the plumb-cut P at once. By applying the square as shown twelve times successively the required length of the rafter and foot-cut B is obtained. In this case the twelve applications of the square are made between the points P and B. Run and rise must also be measured between these points. If run is measured from the point B, which will be the outer edge of the wall plate, it will be necessary to run a gauge line through B parallel to the edge of the rafter, and subtract a distance from the height of the ridge to give us the correct rise. The square must then be applied to the line L. A rafter of any desired rise and run may be laid off in this manner by selecting proportional parts of the rise and run for the blade and tongue of the square. For a half-pitch roof use 12 in. on both tongue and blade, for a quarter-pitch use 6 in. and 12 in., for a third- pitch use 8 in. and 12 in., etc. The terms half-pitch, quarter-pitch, etc., refer to the height of the ridge expressed as a fraction of the span.

The line L is supposed to represent the path of the fence as it is slid along the edge of the rafter. This will be explained at greater length in the following pages.

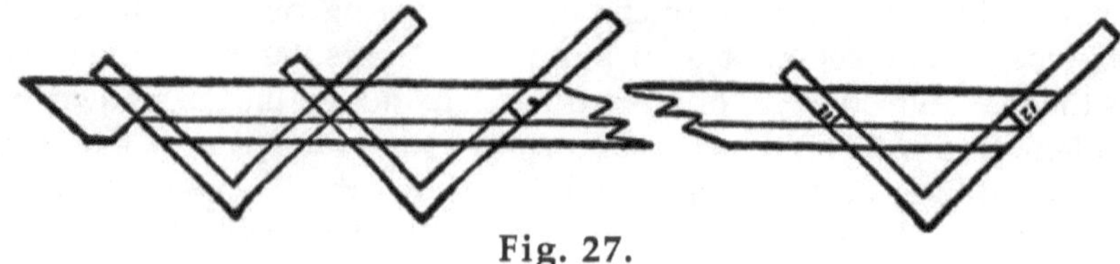

Fig. 27.

At Fig. 27 I show a method of laying out a rafter without making use of a fence. In this case the roof is supposed to be half-pitch, so we take 12 and 12 on the square and apply it to the rafter as many times as there are feet in half the width of the building, which in this case will be 15 feet, as we suppose the building to be 30 feet wide. As the lower end of the rafter is notched to sit on the plate we must gauge off a backing line, as shown, to run into the angle of the notch. This line will be the line on which the gauge points 12 and 12 on the square must start from each time.

Starting from this notch apply the square, keeping the twelve-inch mark on both sides of the square carefully on the backing line, and marking off the rafter on the outside edges of the square. Repeat this until you have fifteen spaces marked off, then set back from your last mark half the thickness of the ridge-board, and with the square as before mark off the rafter. This will be the exact length and also the plumb-cut to fit the ridge-board. Or if we take the diagonal of 12 by 12, which is 17, and mark off 15 spaces of 17 in., making the necessary allowance for the half thickness of the ridge-board, it will amount to the same thing, every 17 in. on the rafter being nearly equal to one foot on the level.

Should the building measure 30 ft., 9 in. in width—the half of which is 15 ft., 4½ in.—we take the fifteen spaces of 12 by 12 and then the 4½ in. on both sides of the square on the backing line as before. This will give us the extra length required. The same rule will apply to any portion of a foot there may be.

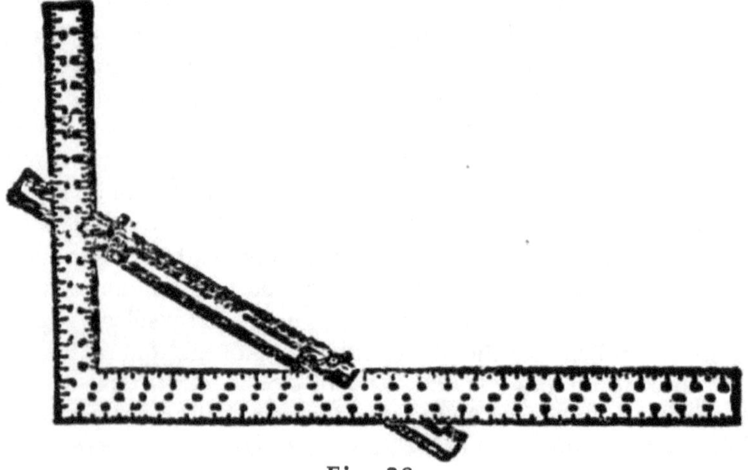

Fig. 28.

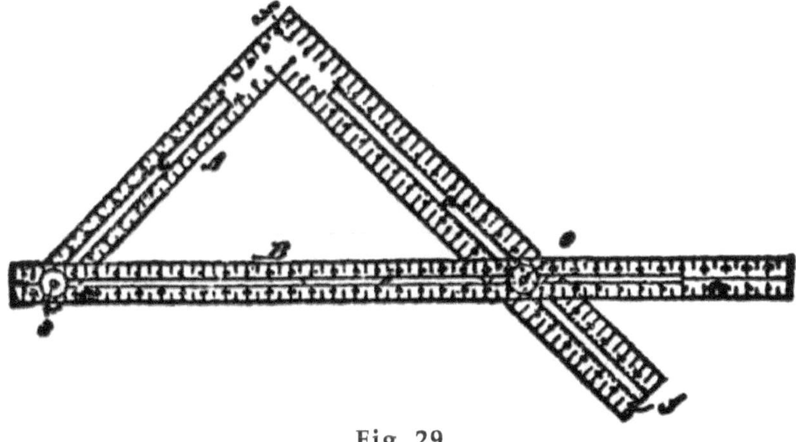

Fig. 29.

A fence, sometimes called a stair gauge, is manufactured of metal by the Cheney & Tower Company, Athol, Mass., which I show at Fig. 28, and is considered about the best thing of the kind. It consists of a piece of polished angle metal, each side being ⅞ inch wide. One side is slotted to accommodate the heads of the set-screws and to allow the slides to be fastened at the desired points. The gauge is fastened to any square and is useful for laying out stairs, cutting in rafters, cutting bevels or other angles. In marking off stairs with an 8-inch rise and an 11¾-inch tread the gauge would be fastened at 8 inches on one end of the square and 11¾ at the other end. The square would then be laid on the plank with the face of the gauge against its edge and the mark made around the point of the square. This would be repeated until the required number of steps were marked. The gauges are made in two sizes, 18 and 28 inches long. It is stated that mechanics who have used it find it one of the handiest tools in their kits.

Another style of fence is shown at Fig. 29 in conjunction with a slotted square. This, perhaps, is the handiest of all the devices for a fence, but it is expensive, and as constructed requires a square with a slot in each arm, and as a rule workmen do not take kindly to squares with slots in them. A shows the square, B the fence, SS set screws to hold the fence in position, and *ff* the points of the square.

The application of the square and fence combined for laying out a housed string for stairs is shown at Fig. 30. In this example the fence is a single slotted one, and three screws are employed to hold the square in position. The rise is seven inches and the tread is laid off nine inches on the blade. The square at the foot of the string shows how the latter should be finished to make the floor and the base- board. In case no pitch-board is required, as the square when adjusted with fence, as shown, does the work of the pitch-board.

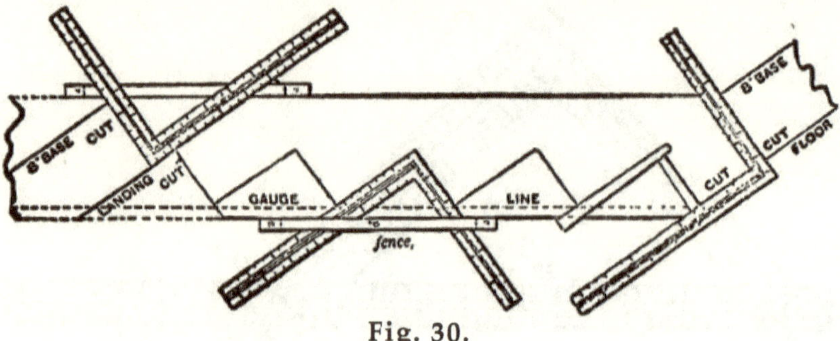

Fig. 30.

There are many other applications of the fence in connection with the square that I may have cause to refer to as I proceed, as it is my desire to present in this work everything I can collect regarding the square that I think will be of service to the workman. Doubtless there will be many descriptions and illustrations some of my readers will have met with before, or which they have been acquainted with for a long time. The great bulk of readers, however, will be new hands and unacquainted with the use of the square beyond its simple application as a squaring tool, and what may appear to be a useless rule to the expert or old hand will prove a choice tidbit to the beginner and will whet his appetite for further knowledge on the subject. Indeed this book is prepared more particularly for the younger members of the craft, although a majority of the older workers will find much in it that will interest, amuse and instruct.

It will be seen that the fence or guide used in connection with the square is, after all, a very simple matter, and would, no doubt, suggest itself to any clever workman who was laying off rafters with the square.

BRACE RULES.

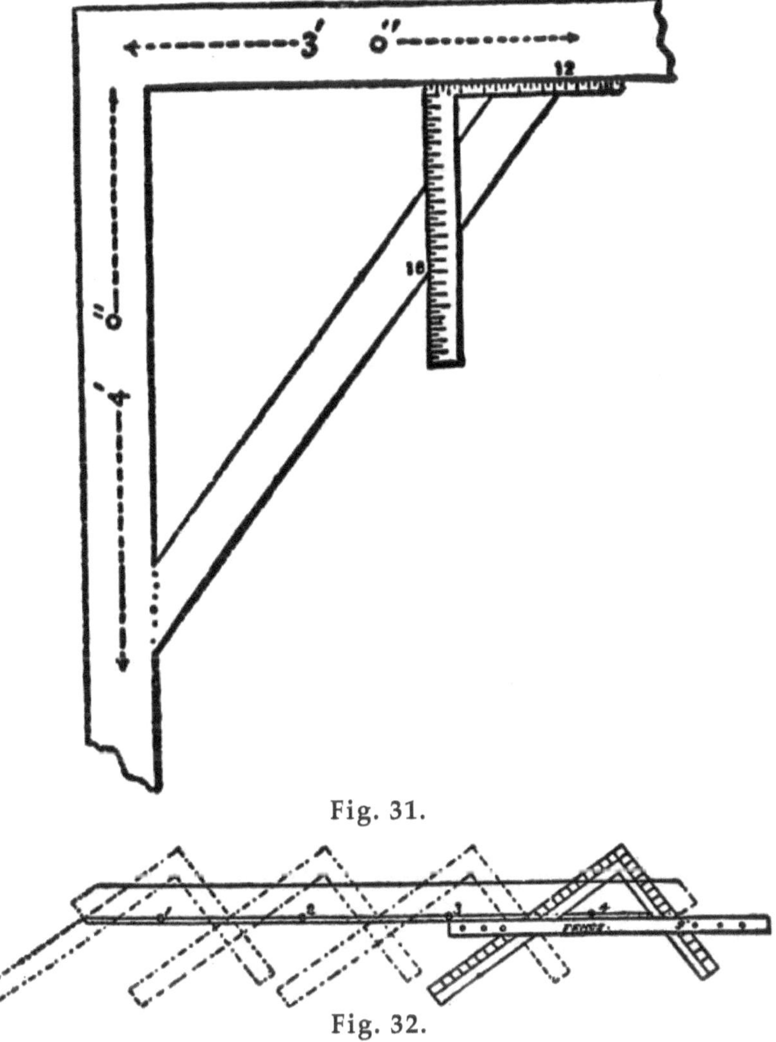

Fig. 31.

Fig. 32.

It will now be in order to show how the square can be used for getting the lengths and bevels for braces of regular and irregular runs. If we wish to lay out a brace having a three-foot run on both post and beam, the matter is quite simple, for we can take 12 inches on the tongue and 12 inches on the blade and transfer this distance three times on a straight line and we have the extreme length of the brace from point to point, and by marking along the blade at one end of this length and along the tongue at the other end we also get the bevels. This is easy and simple enough, and without further refinement will give the lengths and bevels exactly for a flat-footed brace. When the run is different than the rise, as in the example shown at Fig. 31, the square is applied in a somewhat different manner. Here we have a run of three feet and a rise of four feet.

To get the proper length and bevels for a brace to fit in this situation we must use 12 inches on the tongue and 16 inches on the blade, then the bevel of the upper end of the brace will be found along the line of the tongue, and the line of the blade will give the bevel for the foot of the brace. In this case the square is transferred three times, just as though the rise and run were both three feet; the difference being made by dividing the odd foot into three equal parts of 4 inches each and adding one part to the blade, thus making the gauge point on the blade 16 inches instead of 12 inches, which regulates the extra length and the change in bevels. A little study on the part of the reader will reveal to him how the square may be set to gauge points so as to make a brace suitable for any rise and run of any right-angled frame work.

A brace intended for equal run and rise of four feet is shown at Fig. 32. Here we have the fence in use, and the square is shown in all its positions from start to finish in the formation of the brace. The gauge line marked *0000* is the line from which the marks 12 and 12 are supposed to measure, and this when squared over as shown leaves a butt, or "heel of the brace," which is to rest on a shoulder "boxed" in both beam and post. The dotted lines on the ends of the brace show the tenons for which mortises are made in both post and girt or beam. It must be understood, of course, that this operation is only performed once for each kind of brace, and that on a pattern made of some kindly wood, such as pine, cedar or whitewood. For the pattern, dress up a piece of wood to 4 inches wide if the braces are to be made of 4x4-inch stuff; if for larger or smaller stuff then make the pattern the width of brace to suit. Have the pattern of sufficient length; if for a 4-foot run and rise it will require to be not less than 6 feet long. Run a gauge line three-eighths of an inch from the straight or front edge, as shown at 0000, and set the two 12-inch marks on this line, then screw the fence tight on the square with its sliding edge against the edge of the pattern, and then slide and mark as shown four times, when the length and bevels of the brace will be obtained. Provide for the tenons beyond the lines shown by the square, or for a "flat-foot" brace, saw the timber off on the lines shown on the edge of the square. After the pattern is made the fence and square may be laid aside, as the pattern can be used for any number of braces, and when finished with on one job, may be safely placed away to use again for the same "run and rise" when occasion arises. The pattern may be any thickness from half an inch to one inch. The same rules may be observed in making patterns for any regular or irregular runs and rises.

With regard to the *brace rule* as given on steel squares, I may say that there is some slight difference in the lengths given by different makers—though nearly all modern makes figure up alike—but this difference is so small that in soft wood framing it has no effect. In hardwood framing the framer never applies these rules, but gets his lengths with the square and fence.

The length of any brace simply represents the hypothenuse of a right-angled triangle. To find the hypothenuse, extract the square root of the sum of the square of the perpendicular and horizontal runs. For instance, if 6 feet is the horizontal run and 8 feet the perpendicular, 6 squared equals 36, 8 squared equals

64, 36 plus 64 equals 100, the square root of which is 10. These are the figures generally used for squaring the frame of a building or foundation wall.

If the run is 42 inches, 42 squared is 1764, double that amount, both sides being equal, gives 3528, the square root of which is, in feet and inches, 4 feet, 11.40 inches.

In cutting braces always allow in length from a sixteenth to an eighth of an inch more than the exact measurement calls for.

Directly under the half-inch marks on the outer edge of the back of the tongue will be noticed two figures, one above the other. These represent the run of the brace, or the length of two sides of a right- angled triangle; the figures immediately to the right represent the length of the brace or the hypothenuse. For instance, the figures 36-36 59-91 show that the run on the post and beam is 36 inches, and the length of the brace is 50.91 inches.

Upon some squares will be found brace measurements given where the run is not equal, as 18-24 30. It will be noticed that the last set of figures are each just three times those mentioned in the set that are usually used in squaring a building. So if the student or mechanic will fix in his mind the measurements of a few runs, with the length of braces, he can readily work almost any length required.

Take a run, for instance, of 9 inches on the beam and 12 inches on the post. The length of brace is 15 inches. A run, therefore, of 2, 3, 20, or any other number of times the above figures, the length of the brace will bear the same proportion to the run as the multiple used. Thus, if you multiply all the figures by 4 you will have 36 and 48 inches for the run, and 60 inches for the brace, or to remember still more easily, 3, 4 and 5 feet, or 6, 8 and 10 feet.

There are other runs that are just as easily fixed in the mind. 51-inch run, brace 6 feet, 12 hundredths of an inch; 8 feet, 3-inch run, brace 11 feet, 8 inches, etc.

The following examples and explanations on roof framing are simple and easily understood, and cannot fail of being valuable to the young mechanic who aspires to become an expert roof framer. These examples will serve as starters, and in the following volume, which will be issued shortly, more advanced examples will be presented.

ROOFFRAMING.

Roof framing can be done about as many different ways as there are me-chanics. But undoubtedly the easiest, most rapid and most practical is framing with the "square." The following cuts will illustrate several applications of the square as applied to roof framing, and all who are interested in the subject can, by giving it a careful study, be able to frame any ordinary roof the mechanic comes in contact with.

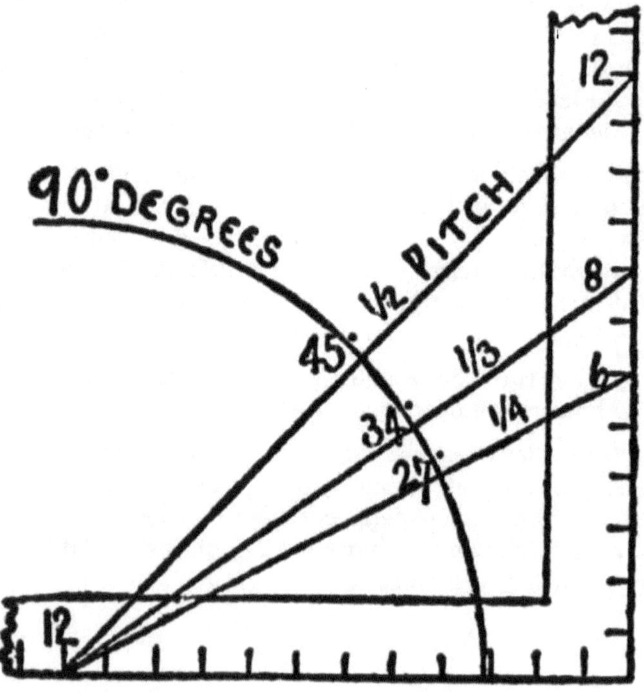

Fig. 33.

Fig. 33 is an illustration that could well be given much thought and study. It not only gives the most common pitches, but also gives the degrees.

Most carpenters know that half-pitch is 45 degrees, yet few know third pitch is nearly 34, and quarter- pitch about 27 degrees.

A building 24 feet wide (as the rafters come to the center) has a 12-foot run and half-pitch the rise would also be 12 feet, and the length of the rafter would be 17 feet (the diagonal of 12). Length, cuts, etc., could all be figured from the one illustration.

Fig. 34.

Fig. 34 illustrates a way to cut rafters with the square.

A roof 14 feet wide would have a run of 7 feet, third-pitch would rise 8 inches to every foot run. Therefore, place the square on 8 and 12 seven times, and you have length and cuts.

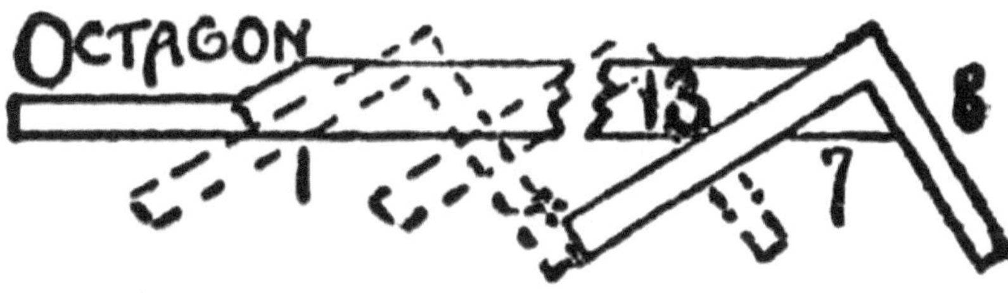

Fig. 35.

Fig. 35. For the octagon rafter, proceed same as common rafter, only use 13 for run (in place of 12 for common rafter).

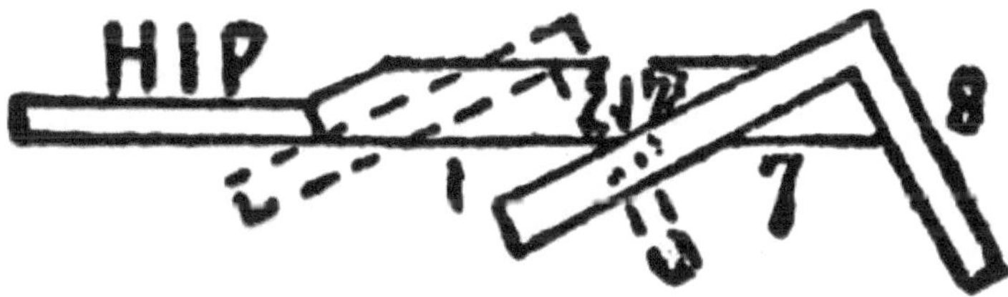

Fig. 36.

Fig. 36, hip or valley rafter. As these rafters run diagonal with the common rafter and as the diagonal of 1 foot is practically 17 inches, use 17 for run, and proceed same as common rafter.

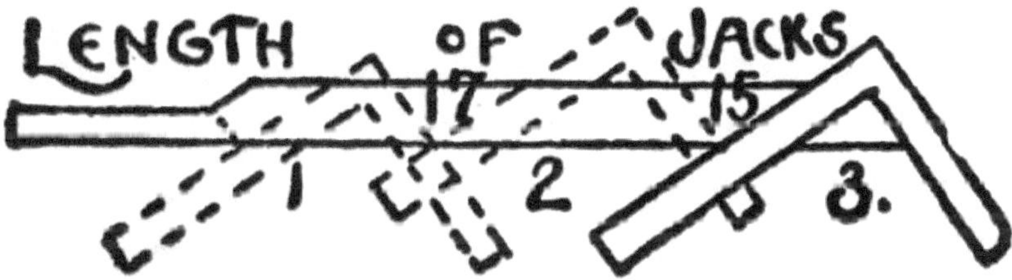

Fig. 37.

Length of jacks. If there are to be five, divide the common rafter into six equal parts, use that for a pattern, and it gives the length very nicely. But that will not always work. To get all the different lengths might at first look difficult even to many good mechanics, but it is very simple as illustrated in Fig. 37. If the first jack was one foot from corner apply the square same as for common rafter, and it gives length and cut (mark the length for starting point on next), and if it is 17 inches from the other move the square up to 17, if the next is 15 move up to 15 and so on.

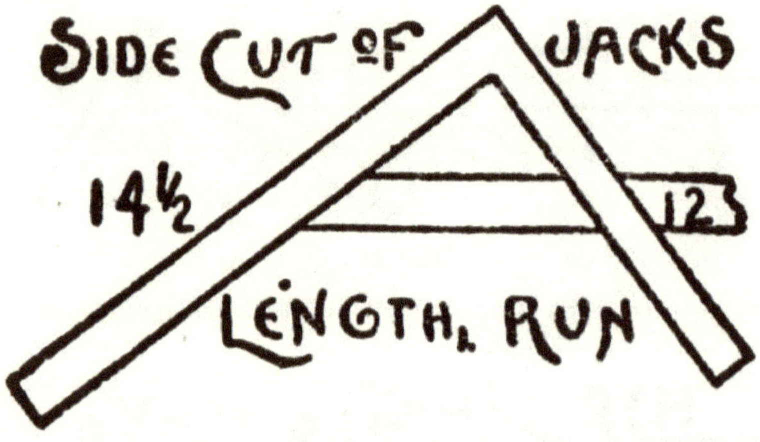

Fig. 38.

Fig. 38. The side cut of jack to fit hip, if laid down level would, of course, be square miter, but the more the hip rises the sharper the angle. Measure across the square from 8 to 12, and it is nearly 14½, which is the length of rafter to one foot of run. Length and run, cut on length, gives the cut.

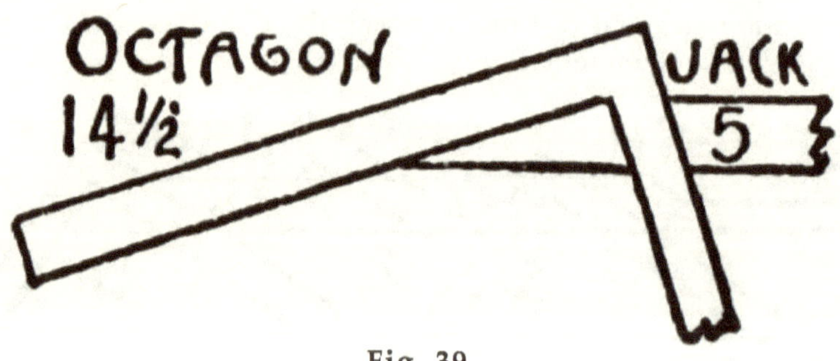

Fig. 39.

Fig. 39, octagon jack. As the octagon miter on level surface is 5 and 12, it must raise same as common jack, and is, therefore, raised to length, or 14½, and 5 cut on length.

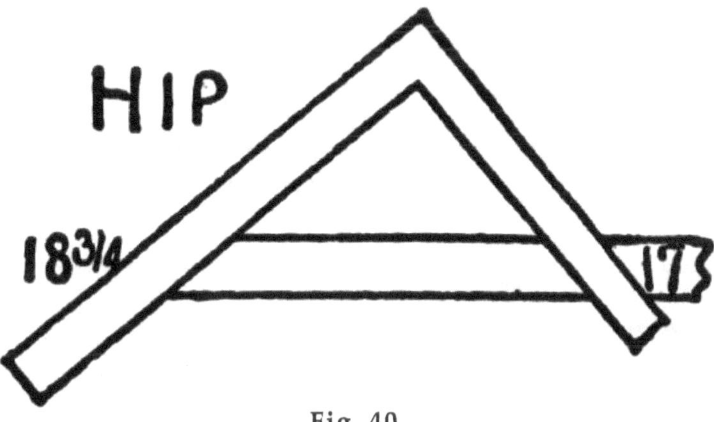

Fig. 40.

Fig. 40, hip rafter, is also length and run, cut on length.

Fig. 41.

Fig. 41. To bevel top of hip take length and rise and mark on rise.

Fig. 42 is another practical way, which is simply to lay the square on heel or hip. The illustration, explains itself.

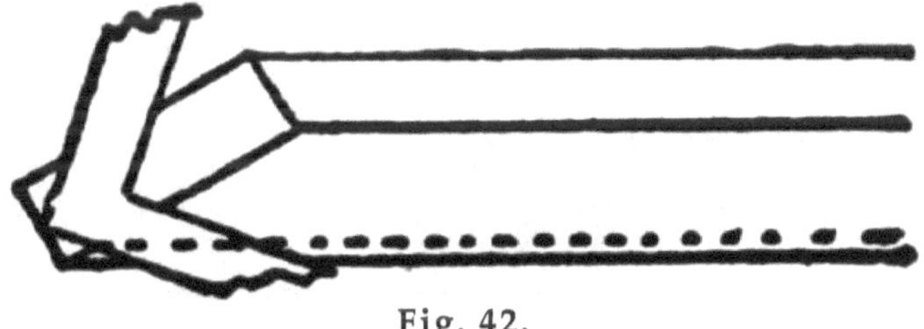

Fig. 42.

Perhaps the most practical way of all to frame a roof, the simplest to understand, easiest to remember, and most rapid to apply is simply to always take the rise and run, measure across the square which gives length. Rise and run give cuts, so you have it all.

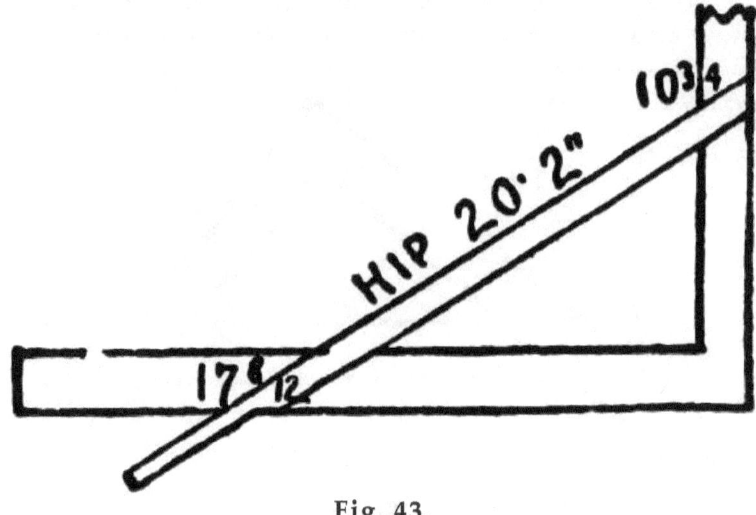

Fig. 43.

Fig. 43 illustrates a roof 25 feet wide and a rise 10 feet, 9 inches, run 12 feet, 6 inches. Measuring across the square from 10¾ to 12½ gives 16½, or 16 feet, 6 inches is the length of rafter.

Fig. 44. If the run of common rafter is 12½, the run of the hip will be diagonal of 12½ which is 17 8- 16, as is plainly illustrated.

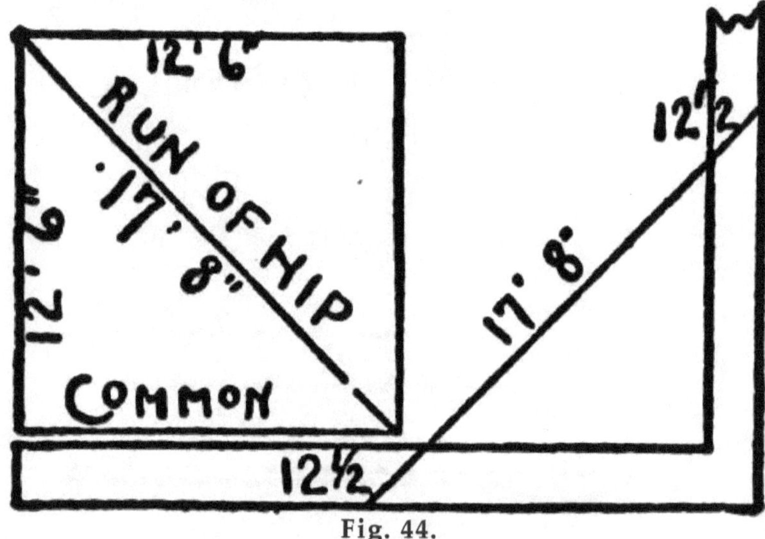

Fig. 44.

Fig. 45. As the rise is 10¾ and run 17 8-12, the length will be 20 feet, 2 inches.

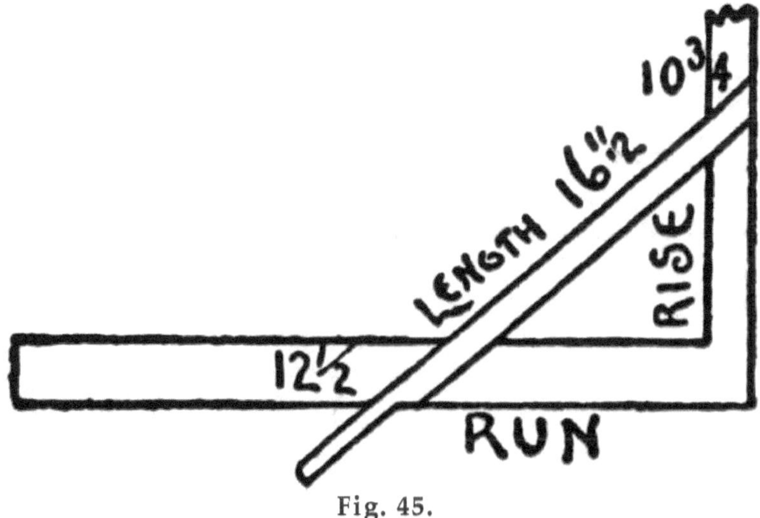

Fig. 45.

Fig. 46. When a roof must go to a certain height to strike another building at a given point, as in additions, porches, etc., don't forget in getting the rise from plate to given point to allow the squaring up of heel as illustrated; and also remember to allow for ridge whenever one is used.

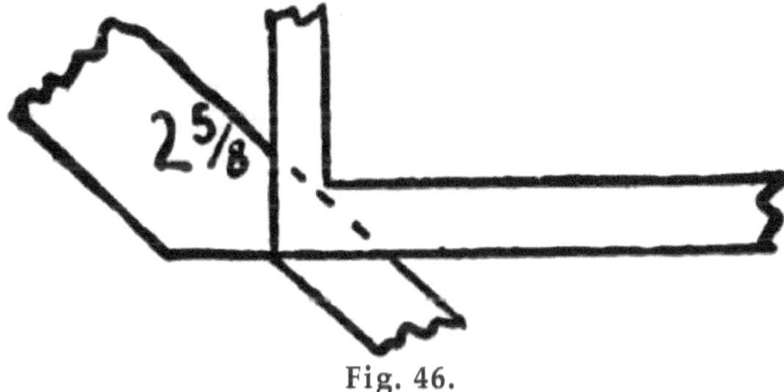

Fig. 46.

Fig. 47 illustrates the cut of top of quarter-pitch rafter to lay on top of roof just mentioned. To apply the square first lay it on 12 and 6, which is quarter-pitch, and gives plumb-cut. From plumb-cut lay off pitch of main roof 10¾ and 12½, which gives cut.

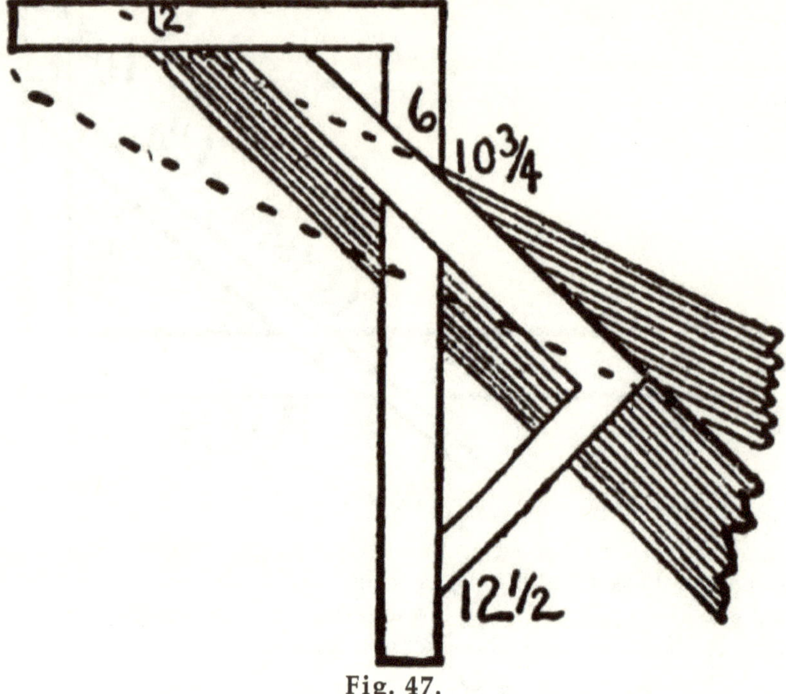

Fig. 47.

Anyone that has studied this with determination will have no trouble in framing any ordinary roof, as the general principles apply to all roofs, pitches, etc. So I will not take up any more space with roof framing at this time, but remember all sheathing, studding, cornice, etc., are made on the same cuts. In fact a hopper is also exactly on the same principle.

DIVISION B

SOME POINTERS ON ROOF FRAMING.

No matter what people may say to the contrary, there is no method or methods that has ever been devised that is so effective in roof framing, or results so rapidly achieved, as those which are obtained by the use of the steel square. I have shown in some of the earlier pages of this work how rapidly the length, and bevels of any common rafter may be obtained by the simple application of the square, any determined number of times. Thus for a building of, say, 30 ft. in width, which is to have a roof of any given pitch, we arrange the pitch as I have shown, with so many inches on the blade for the run, and so many on the tongue for the rise. This settled, we apply the square fifteen times to the rafter, 15 being half of the width of the building. This then gives the length of the rafter, and a line drawn along the edge of the tongue of the square will give the proper bevel for the top or plumb cut. If there is to be a ridge board on the roof, then half the thickness of such board must be measured back on the line drawn, and the rafter must be cut at that point, this provides for the ridge board being nailed on the face of the cut without in the least changing the pitch.

A line along the edge of the blade, gives the proper bevel for the level or horizontal cut. If the bottom end of the rafter is to have a crow-foot cut on it to fit the plate, the workman will have no difficulty whatever in cutting the foot of the rafter to suit, as all the lines will be at right angles to each other, and a section of the plate may be made on the line of the bevel and the "cuts" laid off to suit the conditions.

In reviewing an article of mine on this method of laying out a rafter, an English carpenter took exceptions to it on the grounds that it would take too much time to lay out the rafters for a whole building by this "tiresome process," as he called it. Now the Englishman was right from his point of view, but no American workman would ever think of laying out the rafters for a whole building by the process. He would simply make one rafter as I have shown, for a pattern, and use this pattern for laying out all the other rafters for that particular pitch and rise on the same roof. Most workmen, however, make a pattern from thin stuff of some sort, as it is lighter and easier handled. The reviewer suggested as a better way "that the pitch be arranged on the iron square, then measure across the angle from the points of run and pitch, and multiply this measurement by half the width of the roof to be covered." Now this is all right, but, as a matter of fact, entails more labor of a "tiresome sort" and would use much more time than the method I have taught now for nearly forty years. The American workman, however, does not even require a suggestion as to the quicker method. He will see and adopt it at once without argument.

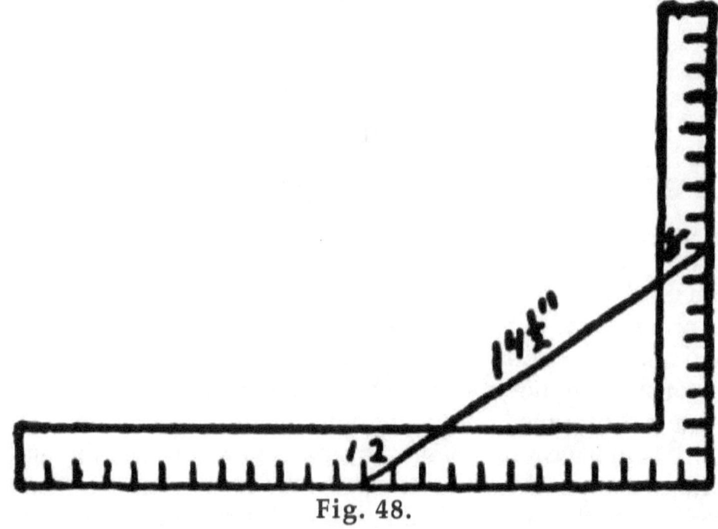

Fig. 48.

The method the Englishman would adopt is shown at Fig. 48, where the points of pitch and run are shown at 12 and 8, which makes the diagonal line 14½ inches. To get the length of the rafter for our supposed building then, we must multiply this 14½ inches fifteen times, then we must use the square at the top and bottom of the timber to obtain the necessary bevels for the cutting lines.

Regarding this question of preparing rafters for a common roof, an "old hand" in the use of the steel square writes to me to say: "I do not think that any simpler method can be given for finding the bevels at the heel and point of rafters than that which you have explained in your books, but I do think that the following method for obtaining lengths of rafters, is somewhat better than yours, particularly when employed for estimating purposes. The most common width of buildings in my locality is 24 ft., and with your permission I purpose to take that width for the practical test of my method. As you have given several ways by which the same result can be obtained, I will ask you to compare them with mine.

Finding the length of the hypothenuse by the old rule, we obtain for one-quarter-inch pitch 13:4.99, or, as near as it can be used on the square 13 feet, 5 inches.

Allowing one inch to the foot and trying your method we find, as a result, 13 inches and 7-16 scant, or 13 feet, 5 inches. This is a very simple method, and when the rule is kept perfectly straight, the results are very satisfactory.

By my way I simply multiply the width of the building by the decimal .56, 24×.56=13.44, or as near as can be worked by the square, 13 feet, 5 inches.

Let us try the same rule for a greater width—say 60 feet. By finding the hypothenuse we find as near as can be used by the square, 33 feet, 6½ inches.

By my method it would be 60×.56, or 33.60, equal to 33 feet, 7 inches full. By this method the rafters in wide buildings are a little long. Thus, if the building is 52 feet wide, by the hypothenuse it would be 29 feet, 1 inch; my way it would be 29 feet, 1½ inches. I consider this an advantage, as it leaves the point of the rafter very slightly open.

For one-third I follow the same plan, only using the decimal .6. Unlike the decimal used for a quarter pitch the lengths are a very small fraction short; as, for instance, a rafter for a building 60 feet wide, by finding the hypothenuse, would be 36 feet, 1-16 of an inch. By my way, 60×.6=36 feet. A slight difference, truly. If building is 48 feet wide, then by the first method we find 28 feet, 10 inches full; by my way, 28 feet, 9⅜ inches. A little practice will enable the mechanic to allow just enough to make up for the slight difference, so that when rafters are put together the fit will be perfect.

The one-half pitch can be found in the same manner by using the decimal .71. Taking the 24-foot building, length of rafters by the hypothenuse, we find 16 feet, 11 2-3 inches; my way they would be 17 feet full. Again, building 60 feet wide, rafters by the first method would be 42 feet, 6⅛ inches; by my way 60×.71=42 feet, 6 inches. By using this decimal, the length is so near practically correct, that it may be used in all cases.

For a full pitch use the decimal 1.12, and as in the preceding mentioned pitch, and it will be found so near correct that it can be practically used in all cases.

It will be noticed that I have not made any allowance for projection of rafters over the plate. In this case gauge from the crowning side of your rafter the thickness of your projection; allow enough for the latter, and find the lower bevel according to the way you described in your last; measure the length of your rafter from where this bevel crosses the gauge line.

A little practice will enable the mechanic to lay off a rafter in a very short time. I have used the above myself, and have no trouble whatever. While I have no fault to find in your methods, as I know them to be correct, yet it is just as well that workmen should know other methods, as there are many occasions when the "only method" he possesses cannot be applied. Hence I submit the foregoing, at your request.

W. H."

All this is very true, and right as far as it goes, but it so happens that many workmen do not have the necessary learning to work out these problems in footing on the lines laid down by W. H., but, in order to meet conditions of this kind I have prepared a series of tables which is inserted in the larger volumes, giving the length of rafters for any building having a width of from five to sixty feet and a rise of roof of from one to eighteen feet to ridge. This will cover the whole ground, and form a ready table for the estimator to take his quantities from.

I may be pardoned for again showing the common and simplest method of laying out an ordinary rafter, for notwithstanding all I have said and described and explained on this subject, there will always be some persons who will not be able to grasp the method, unless it is put to them in some other light. I am sure of this from the long experience I have had in the answering of questions of this kind through the columns of different building journals. This is no doubt owing to some constitutional peculiarities of both the person who makes the inquiry and the person who attempts to answer it. This is one of the main reasons why I have admitted into this work various methods and descriptions of others than myself, so that readers will have the same methods described and explained to them in several different ways by several writers.

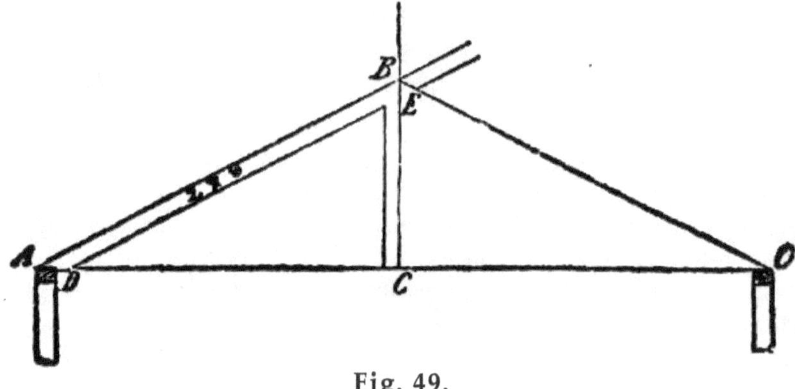

Fig. 49.

Let us take the diagrams shown at Fig. 49, which shows a portion of a roof having a quarter pitch. CEB showing the height, and AB the length and inclination of rafter. D shows the foot of the rafter on the plate, cut "flat foot" and the line EC the plumb cut. This is quite plain. The building may be any width, let us say in this case, that it is 30 feet wide from A to O. That will make the distance from A to C 15 feet.

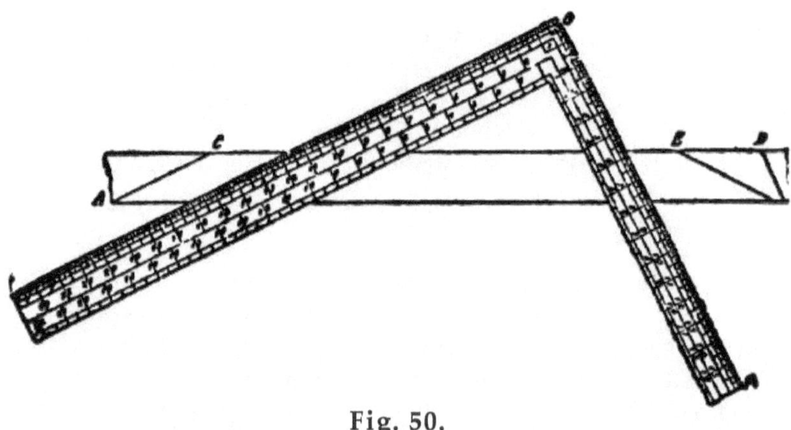

Fig. 50.

A method of obtaining the bevels for this rafter is given in Fig. 50 where the steel square is shown laid on the pattern with the points 16 inches on the blade and 8 inches on the tongue applied to the edge of the stuff. The line HO on the blade gives the bevel for the foot of the rafter AC. The line OP, Fig. 50 gives the bevel for the top of the rafter or the plumb cut, as most workmen call it. Now, there is nothing in this diagram, which is from Bell's Carpentry, an excellent work—from which the workman can get the length of his rafter, without complicating matters. Had the figures 12 inches and 6 inches on the square been employed instead of 16 and 8, then the distance across the diagonal from these two points would have equalled on the rafter, one foot on the base line or seat of the rafter, so that 15 times that length would have been the total length of the rafter. Better still, however, would have been the application of the square 15 times on the edge of the rafter pattern with the points 12 and 6 on gauge points, then both length and bevels would have been obtained at one operation.

Of course, the expert workman will often invent, or discover, methods of using the square in certain phases of roof framing, that can not be found in books, or that cannot be taught because of the peculiar circumstances of the particular case. Having a fair knowledge of the uses of the steel, the workman will seldom be overtaken by difficulties he cannot overcome if he studies the problems before him and then employs his knowledge of the square to their solution, as a little application on this line will remove all possible troubles.

Every carpenter knows, or ought to know, that the run and rise of the rafter taken on the square will give the seat and plumb cuts, but inasmuch as buildings are not all of the same width, it requires a different set of figures for each run, and as it requires an extra calculation to first find the run of the hip or valley, it is better to use the full scale for a one-foot run of the common rafter which answers for any run.

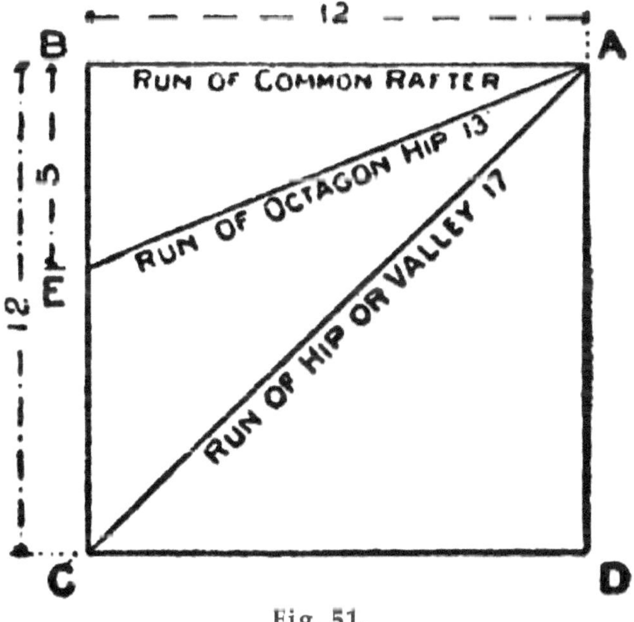

Fig. 51.

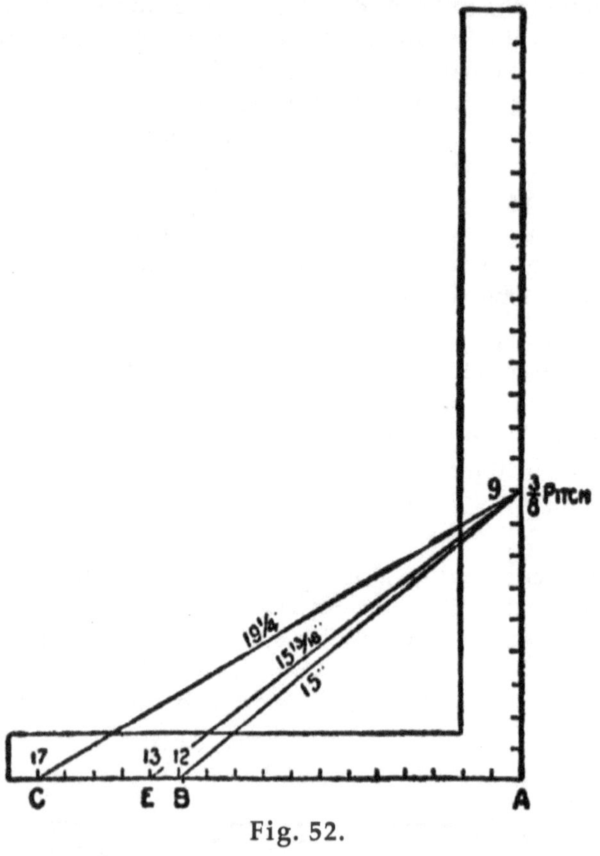

Fig. 52.

Referring to Fig. 51, we show a square bounded by A, B, C, D, the sides of which are 12 inches. E is at a point 5 inches from B, and C 12 inches from B. B-A represents the run of the common rafter. E-A represents the run of the octagon hip or valley, and C-A the same for the common hip or valley, their lengths, being 12, 13, and 17 respectively. Now since 12, 13, and 17 are fixed numbers, we take them on the tongue of the square, as shown in Fig. 52. Now suppose we want to find the lengths and cuts of the rafters for the ⅜ pitch. We take 9 on the blade. Why? Because the run being 12 inches, the span must be two times 12, which equals 24, and since the pitch is reckoned by the span, we find that ⅜ of 24 is 9, which represents the rise of the foot run. Then 12 and 9 give the seat and plumb cuts for the common rafter, 13 and 9 for the octagon hip or valley, and 17 and 9 gives the same for the common hip or valley. In Fig. 53 I show each separately.

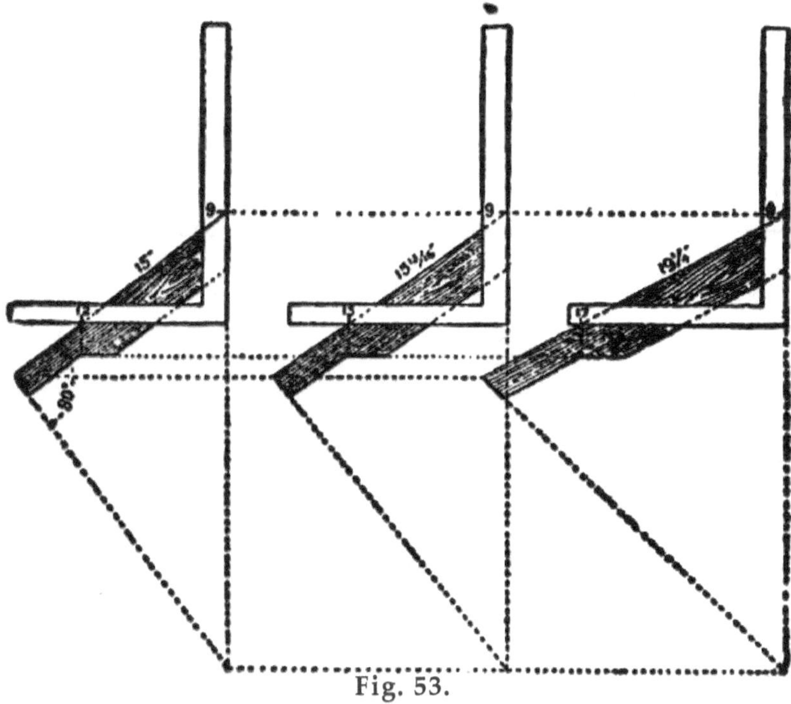
Fig. 53.

The measurement line of hips and valleys is at a line along the center of its back, and just where to place the square on the side of the rafter so as to make the cuts and length come right at that point is a question that taxes the skill of most carpenters, especially so when the rafters are so backed. In Fig. 54 I have tried to make the above points clear.

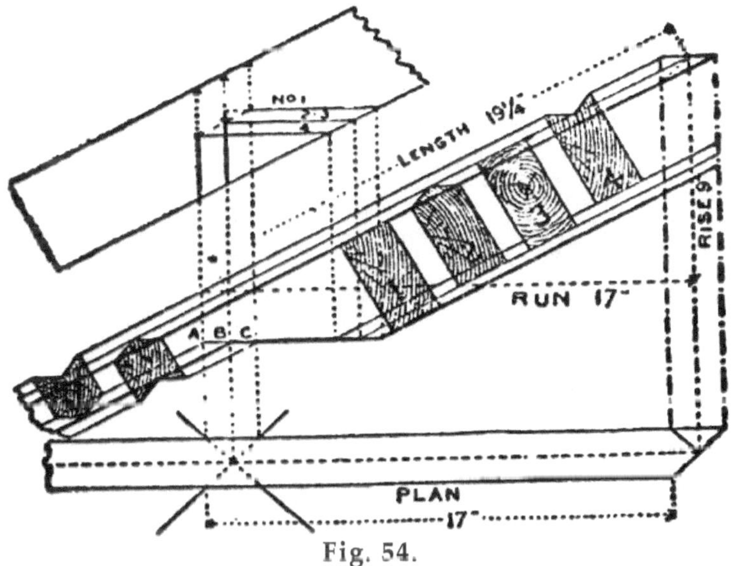

Fig. 54.

First, I show the plan of the rafter. The cross lines on same represent an external corner for the hip and valley respectively. Above the plan is shown the elevation. The sections 1-2-3-4 represent the position of the rafters under the following conditions: No. 1 hip when not backed, No. 2 hip when backed, No. 3 valley when not backed, No. 4 valley when backed. No. 1 is outlined by heavy lines, and sets lower than the others. By tracing the bottom line of the sections down to the seat of No. 1, thence up to the second elevation will show just how deep the notching should be for each rafter. No. 1 cuts into the right hand vertical line from the plan, which would make it stand at the right height above the plate, but in order to make the seat cut clear the corner of plate, it is necessary to cut into the center line above the plan. No. 2 cuts into the same points as No. 1, but owing to its being backed, the seat cut drops accordingly. No. 3 cuts into the center vertical line, and in order to clear the edges of the plate must cut out at the sides to the left vertical line. No. 4 cuts in the same as the latter, but as much lower than No. 3 as No. 2 is below No. 1.

The outer vertical lines from the plan represent the width of the rafter. Therefore if the rafter be two inches thick, would be one inch apart, and this amount set off along the seat line (or a line parallel with it) will give the gauge point on the side of the rafter. To make this clearer refer to Fig. 53; 17 and 9 gives the cuts. Now leaving the square rest as it is, measure back from 17 one-half the thickness of the rafter, and this will be the gauge line point from which to remove the wood back to the center line of hip, and the measurement from the edge of the rafter taken vertically down to the gauge point set off on the plumb cut regulates how far apart the parallel lines of the seat cuts will be under the above conditions. This rule applies to any roof so long as the pitches are regular.

Proceed in like manner for the octagon hip, the variation, however, is practically one-half of the above results for the square cornered building.

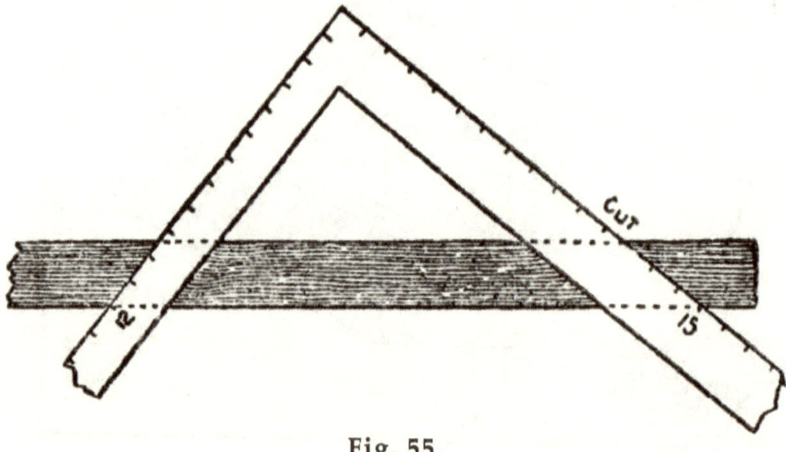

Fig. 55.

Fig. 55 illustrates side cut of the jack, 12 on the tongue, and 15 (length of the common rafter) on the blade.

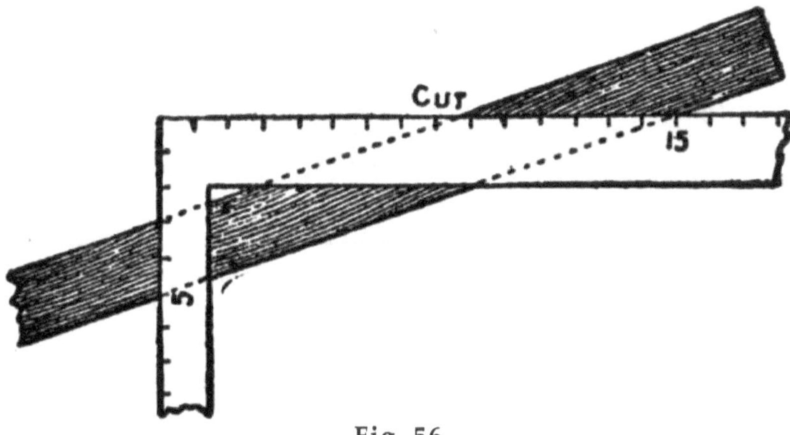

Fig. 56.

Fig. 56 illustrates side cut of the octagon jack, 5 on the tongue and 15 on the blade.

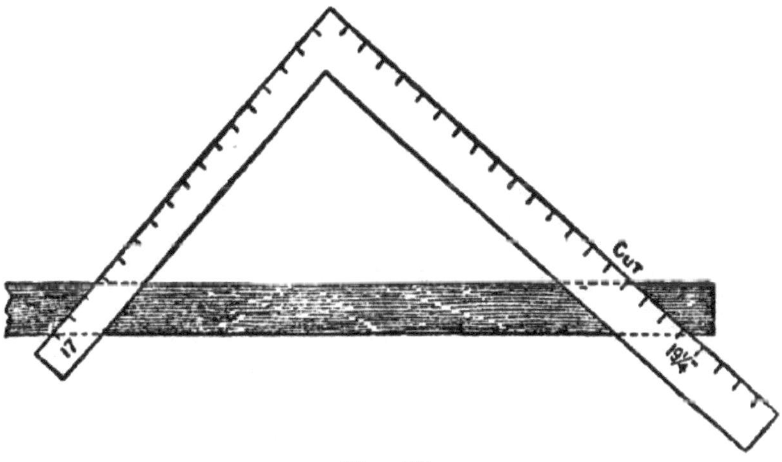

Fig. 57.

Fig. 57 illustrates the side cut of the hip or valley, 17 on tongue, 19¼ (length of the hip) on the blade giving the cut in each case.

The latter, however, is for the unbacked rafter. If it has been previously backed, then apply the square with the above figures on the lower edge at bottom of the plumb cut, or apply the square as for the jack, Fig. 56, to the backing line, which will give the same result as 17 and 19¼.

It is quite clear that when a workman cuts a common rafter, he is also cutting a timber that would answer for a hip for a building of less span having the same rise, only taking some adjustment of the top bevel to fit against a ridge. This is quite plain, and if we refer to Fig. 58, we find that the common rafter for a 1-foot run becomes a hip for an 8½-inch run, and that a hip for a 1-foot run of the building becomes a common rafter for a 17-inch run. Therefore, the rule that applies to the common rafter also applies to the hip rafter, *i. e.,* the run and rise taken on the square will give the seat and plumb cuts. The run and length of the rafter taken on the square will give the side cuts, or taking the scale for a 1-foot run, Fig. 58, it is 12 on the tongue and the rise on the blade for the common rafter, and 17 on the tongue and rise on the blade for the hip. The tongue giving the seat cut and the blade the plumb cut. For the side cuts we take 12 on the tongue and 15⅝ inches on the blade, and the blade will give the side cut of the jack. Take 17 on the tongue and the length of the hip, 19¾ inches, on the blade and the blade will give the side cut of the hip. It would also be the side cut of the corresponding jack if it be a common rafter. Seventeen is used for a foot run of the hip rafter because the diagonal of a 12-inch square is practically 17 inches.

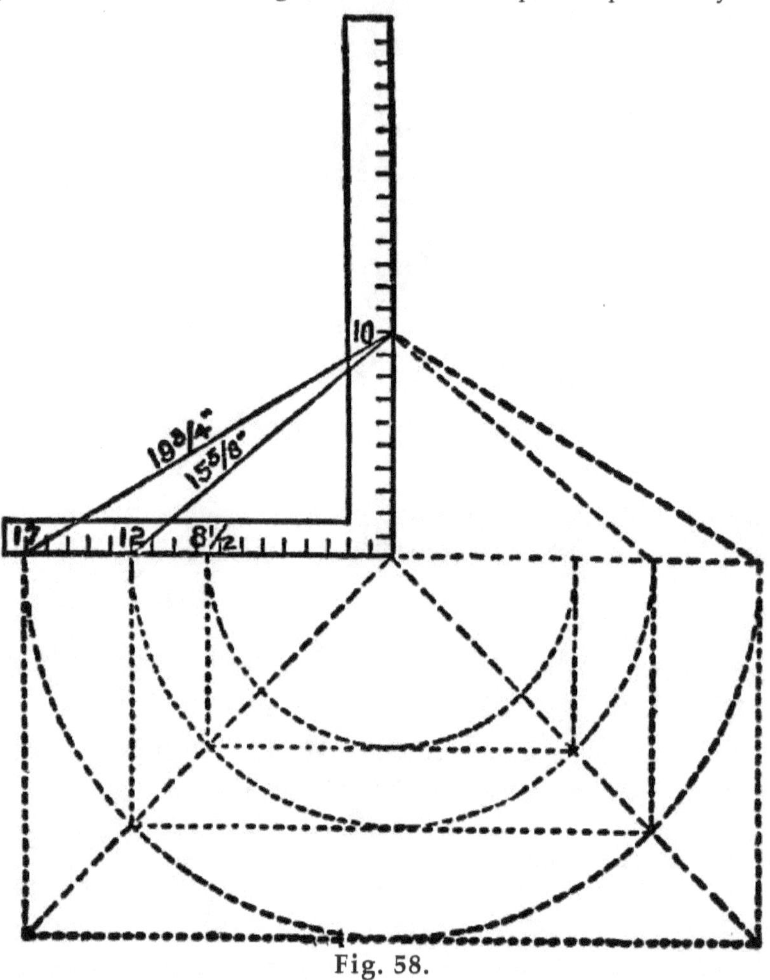

Fig. 58.

If we were to use 12 on the tongue for a foot run of the hip the rise to the foot would necessarily be less than 10 inches. In Fig. 59 I show what the difference is in rise to the foot.

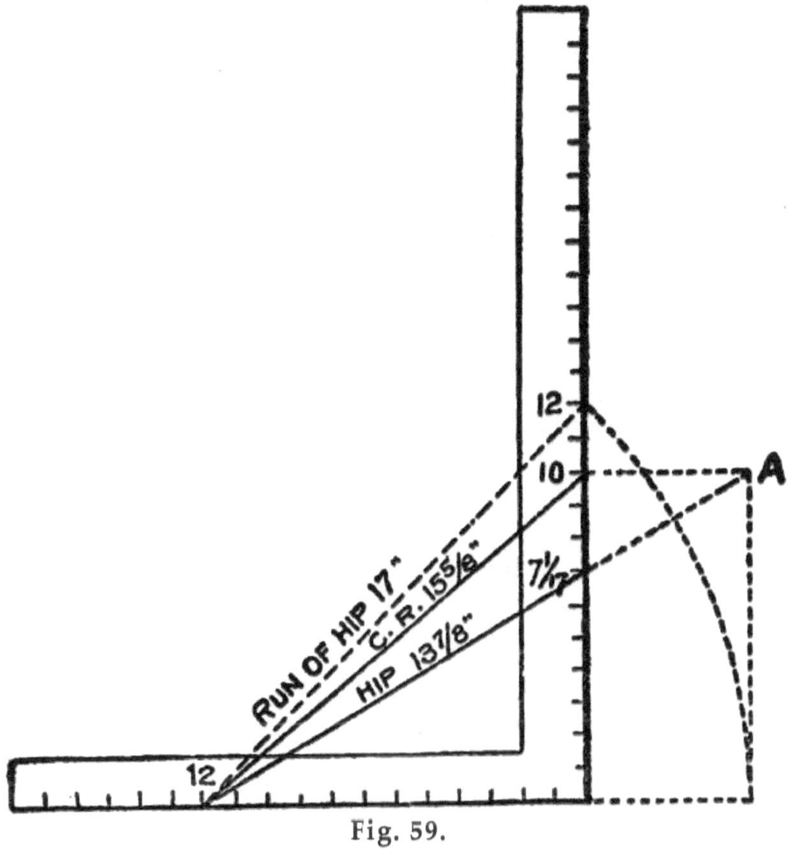

Fig. 59.

From 12 to 12 is the length of the run of the hip would only have 10-17 of an inch to one run of the common rafter, and an equal rise of the common rafter, set off as at A, and a line from this to 12 on the tongue passes at 7 1-17 inches on the blade, because the common rafter having a rise of 10 inches to one foot, for one inch it would have 10-12 of an inch, while the hip would only have 10-17 of an inch to one inch and for 12 inches it would be 12 times 10-17 equals 120-17, or 7 1-17 inches. Therefore the figures given in the second illustration would give the same cuts as those in the first, but as the latter necessitates a calculation that ends in fractions—fractions not given on the square—and for that reason 17 is generally used for a foot run for the hips and valleys.

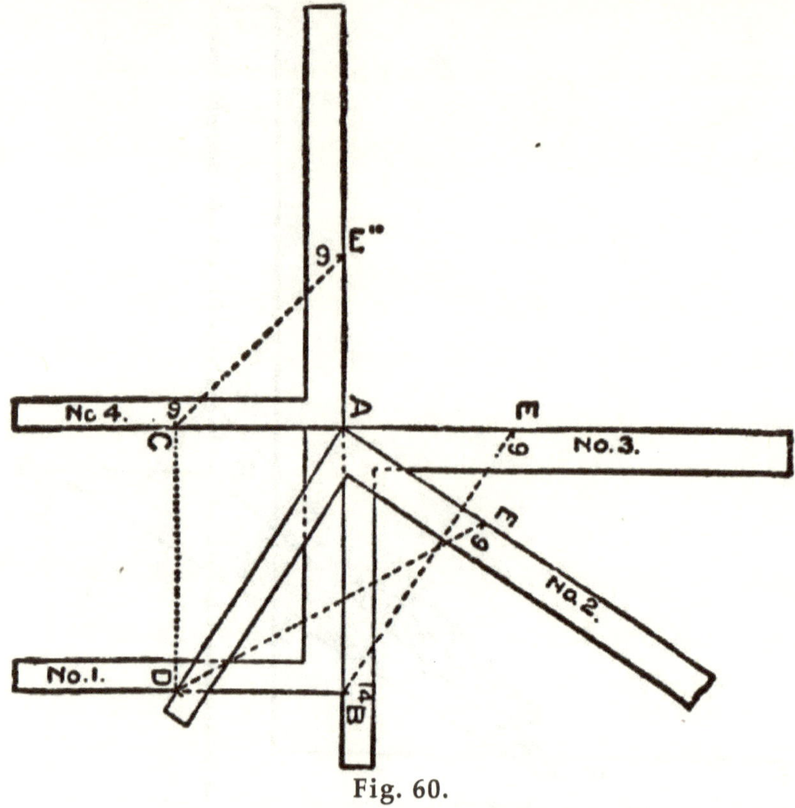

Fig. 60.

AN UNEQUAL PITCH.

In the matter of roofing over unequal pitches when there is no ridge and when all hips meet, the building being longer than it is wide, the backing of hips and their lengths and bevels would be a very easy matter if a drawing of the whole thing was made, but, to obtain these by the use of the square alone, is somewhat more difficult. Let us assume the building to be 18 feet wide and 28 feet long, and having a rise of 9 feet, then, by referring to Fig. 60, we show to one inch scale the length, run, rise, seat, and plumb cuts for the hip and common rafters as follows: The run of the long way of the building is 14, and 9 for the narrow way, which we take on the blade and tongue respectively, as shown on square No. 1, and to this apply square No. 2, as shown. AD equals the run of the hip. AE equals the rise and ED equals the length of the hip. The reader will notice that the letters A, B, C, D form a parallelogram, with side and ends equal to the runs of the common rafters. Therefore, by taking the runs on the tongue, as shown by the squares Nos. 3 and 4, will give their lengths, seat and plumb cuts.

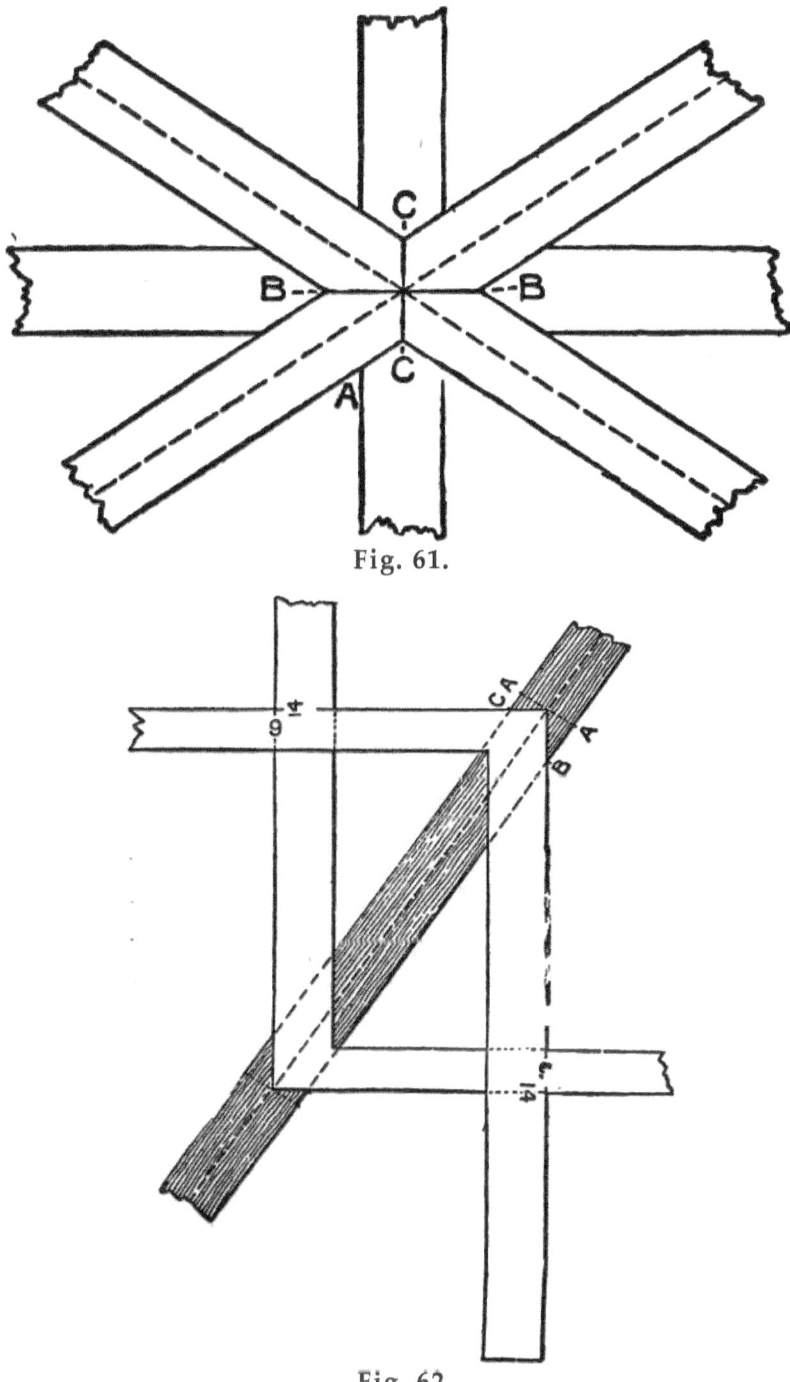

Fig. 61.

Fig. 62.

In Fig. 61 is shown the intersection of the rafters at the peak and as the
lengths of all rafters are scaled to run to a common center it is necessary that the

common rafters must cut back so as to fit in the angle formed by the hips. The proper deduction for this is shown in Fig. 62 by placing two squares on the back of the rafter, with the heel or corner of the squares resting on the center line. The distance from the corner of the square to B measured square back (at right angles) from the plumb bevel, as shown in Fig. 61, will locate the point of the long common rafter at B in Fig. 61. Proceed in like manner for the short common rafter, taking the distance from the corner at C, and for the side cuts, take 14 on the tongue and the length of the short common rafter CE on the blade—the blade will give the cut at AC in Fig. 61. The reader will observe that this angle is the same as that for the side cut of the jack. Proceed in like manner for the long common rafter side, using 9 on the tongue and BE on the blade. These same figures will give the side cuts of the hip, provided hip has been previously backed. Taking the last for example the reader will observe that 9 on the tongue and BE on the blade the square would lay on the plane of the backing and the blade giving the cut along the line BB in Fig. 61, or these cuts may be found by measuring square back from a plumb bevel at points A and A, Fig. 62, the distance AC and AB, which will give the proper plumb cut at the sides and intersecting the line AA at the center. These same distances, AC and AB, but transferred to opposite sides, set off on the seat cut or a line parallel with it, will give the gauge points on the side of the hip for the backing.

The lengths of the jacks may be found by dividing the length of the common rafter by the number of the spacings for the jacks; the quotient will be the common difference.

END OF DIVISION B.

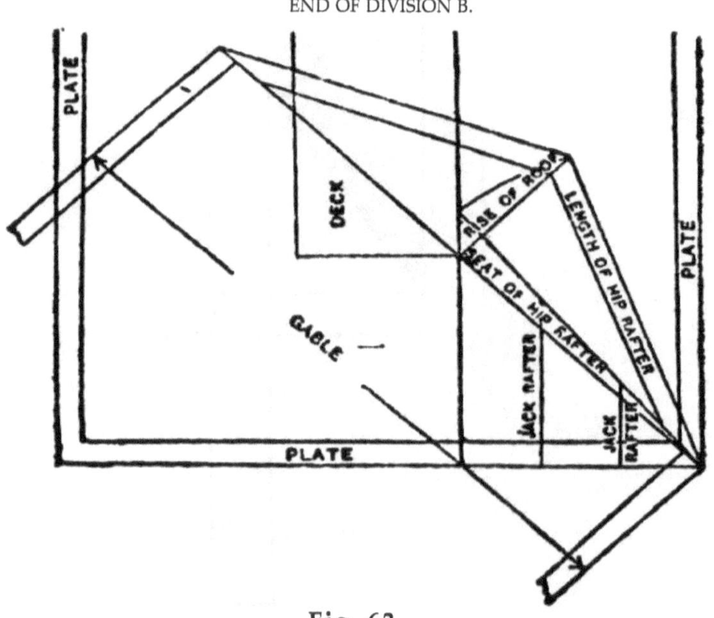

Fig. 63.

LAY-OUT OF HIP-ROOF WITH DECK.

THE STEEL SQUARE AND ITS USES.

DIVISION C.

INTRODUCTORY.

During my long experience as Editor of several of the leading building journals in the United States and Canada, I have been asked and have answered thousands of questions regarding matters concerning building construction, builders' materials, tools and processes, and particularly regarding the "Steel Square and its Uses," and I have concluded that the publication of a few of these questions and answers, along with other matter, in this division will be appreciated by my readers, and to this end I insert a number of the most useful items in this manual.

Besides these questions and answers, I also publish other up to date matter, all of which will make this volume one of the most useful little works to the American carpenter and wood-worker ever published.

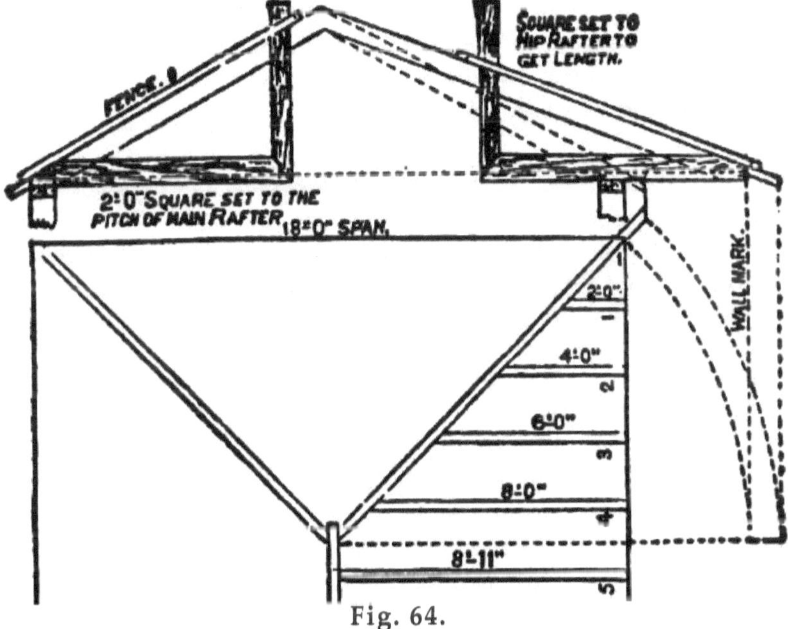

Fig. 64.

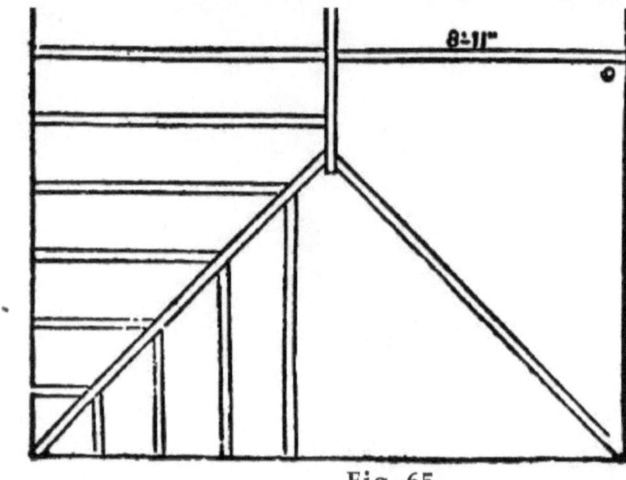

Fig. 65.

I open this division with a few hints regarding the construction, or rather the laying out of a Hip-Roof where the design has been furnished by an architect, and which, of course, shows the pitch and the lay of the timbers. We suppose the roof to have a span of 18 feet and a rise of 6 feet, thus giving the roof a one-third pitch. The fence is used in this example to its full extent, and when placed on the square and fastened, the line of fence shows the slope or pitch of roof. Fig. 64 shows the square set to the pitch of the hip rafter. The squares as set give the plumb and level cuts. Fig. 65 is the rafter plan of a house 18 by 24 feet; the rafters are laid off on the level, and measure nine feet from center of ridge to outside of wall; there should be a rafter pattern with a plumb cut at one end, and the foot cut at the other, got out as previously shown. When the rafter foot is marked, place the end of the long blade of the square to

the wall line, as in drawing, and mark across the rafter at the outside of the short blade, and these marks on the rafter pitch will correspond with two feet on the level plan; slide the square up the rafter and place the end of the long blade to the mark last made, and mark outside the short blade as before, repeat the application until nine feet are measured off, and then the length of the rafter is correct; remember to mark off one-half the thickness of ridge-piece. The rafters are laid off on part of plan to show the appearance of the rafters in a roof of this kind, but for working purposes the rafters 1, 2, 3, 4, 5 and 6, with one hip rafter, is all that is required.

To proceed, we first lay off common rafter, which has been previously explained; but deeming it necessary to give a formula in figures to avoid making a plan, we take 1-3 pitch. This pitch is 1-3 the width of the building, to point of rafter from wall plate or base. For an example, always use 8, which is 1-3 of 24, on tongues for altitude; 12, ½ the width of 24, on blade for base. This cuts common rafter. Next is the hip-rafter. It must be understood that the diagonal of 12 and 12 is approximately 17 in framing work, and the hip is the diagonal of a square added to the rise of roof; therefore we take 8 on the tongue and 17 on the blade;

run the same number of times as common rafter which gives the length of hip and plumb and level bevels.

To cut jack rafters, divide the number of openings for common rafters. Suppose we have five jacks, with six openings, our common rafter 12 feet long, each jack would be 2 feet shorter. The first, next the hip, 10 feet, the second 8 feet, third 6 feet, and so on. The top down cut same as down cut for common rafter. For the bevel, cut against hip. Take half the width of building on tongue and length of common rafter on blade, and blade gives the bevel. Now find diagonal of 8 and 12, which is 14 7-16 in. Take this length on blade and 12 on tongue, blade gives bevels. If the hip-rafter is beveled or "backed" to suit jacks, then take height of hip on tongue, length of hip on blade, and tongue gives bevel. These figures will cover all bevels for cutting, cornice and sheathing. For bed moulds for gable to fit under cornice, take half width of building on tongue, length of common rafter on blade; blade gives cut. To cut planceer to run up valley, take height of rafter on tongue, length of rafter on blade; tongue gives bevel. For plumb cut, take height of hip on tongue, length of hip on blade; tongue gives bevel.

These figures were specially prepared for a hip roof having a one-third pitch, but will suit other pitches equally well if the difference in height of ridge is considered.

For a hopper the mitre is cut on the same principle. To make a butt joint, take the width of side on blade, and half the flare on tongue: the latter gives the cut. You will observe that a hip-roof is the same as a hopper inverted. The cuts for the edges of the pieces of a hexagonal hopper are found this way. Subtract the width of one piece at the bottom from the width of same at top, take remainder on tongue, depth of side on blade; tongue gives the cut. The cut on face of sides: Take 7-12 of the rise on tongue and the depth of side on blade; tongue gives cut. The bevel of top and bottom: Take rise on blade, run on tongue; tongue gives cut.

SOME QUESTIONS AND ANSWERS FROM VARIOUS COR-RESPONDENTS.

The following questions and answers from practical workmen are considered among the very best things regarding the use of the Steel Square, as they are from men who knew of what they were talking about. They are gathered from many sources, but chiefly from the columns of Technical Journals with which I have been connected, either as Editor or contributor.

Jas. Willis, Rochester, N. Y., asks: "How can I get the proper bevel for a butt joint on an obtuse or acute angle, by the use of the square only?"

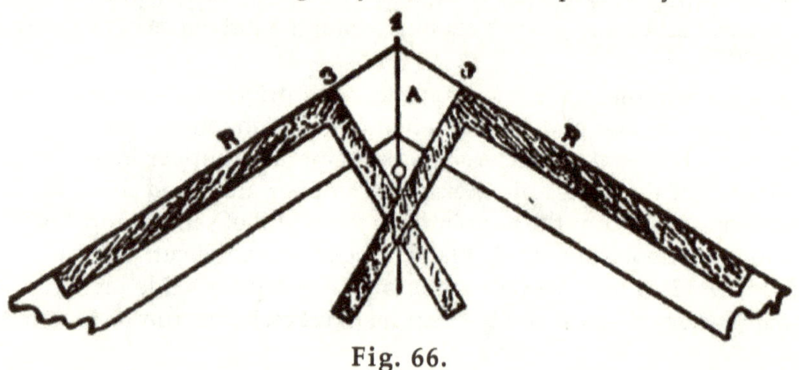

Fig. 66.

Answer: Suppose Fig. 66 represents an obtuse angle formed by two parallel boards or timbers. To obtain the joint, A, space off equal distances from the point 1 to 3, 3, then square over from the lines, R, R, keeping the heel of the square at the points 3, 3. At the junction of the lines formed by the tongue of the square at 0 will be one point, and 1 will be the other by which the joint line, A, is defined.

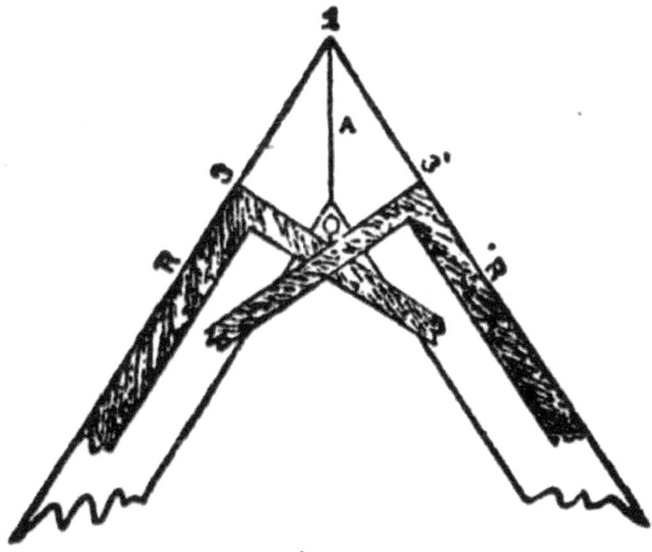

Fig. 67.

To find the line of juncture for an acute angle, proceed as follows: Fig. 67 represents two parallel boards or timbers; 1 the extreme angle, 3, 3 equal distances from the angle 1 and are the points where the heel of the square must rest to form the lines 0, 3; 0 shows the junction of the lines formed by the blade of the square. Draw a line from 0 to 1, and the line, A, formed, is the bevel required.

It will be seen, by these two examples, that the bevel of a junction at any angle may be obtained by this method.

P. McVity, Milwaukee, asks: "How can I draw a circle with the Steel Square?"

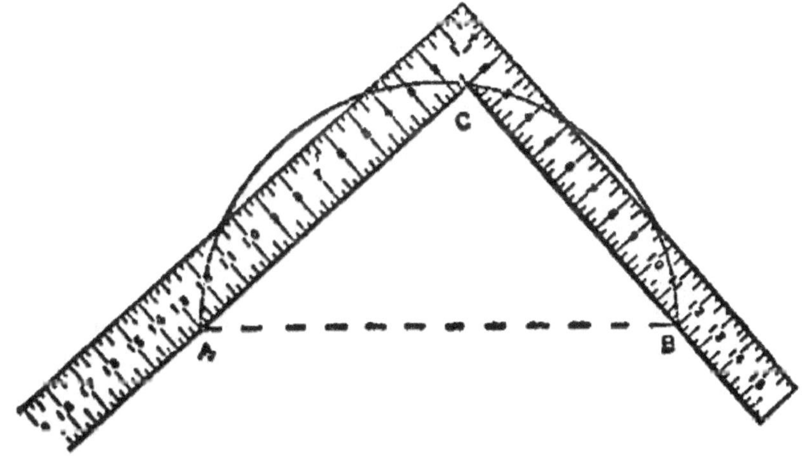

Fig. 68.

Answer: A circle of any required diameter may be drawn by means of the square by using it as indicated in the accompanying sketch. Drive two pins or nails, A and B, Fig. 68, at whatever distance apart the circle is to have as its diameter. Bring the square against them, as shown, and use a pencil in the angle as indicated in the drawing. This rule is very convenient in many instances. Suppose A and B are two points through which a circle is required to be drawn. By bringing the square against pins or nails placed in the points, it may be described as indicated in the sketch.

A "Mechanic," Tampa, Fla., asks: "Can the steel square be used in laying out a wreath for a handrail, and if so, please describe how?"

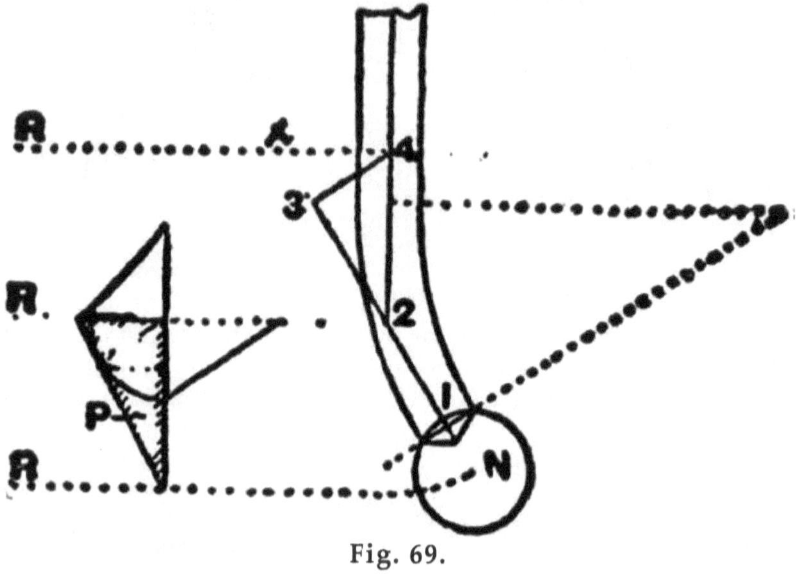

Fig. 69.

Answer: Some advance in this direction has been made, but not much, but the outlook is quite encouraging as many experts are trying to obtain all the lines required for forming circular handrails. It will be accomplished sooner or later. A few problems and solutions are given herewith: In getting out face-molds it has generally been considered necessary first to unfold the tangents and get the heights, and by construction get the bevels. The method shown is somewhat different, though results are the same, but are produced more rapidly. Take for illustration a side wreath mitered into a newel cap. This method will apply no matter where the newel is placed, or whether the easement is less or more than the one step of the example illustrated. What is meant by one step is, that the tangent of the straight rail continues to the point 2, Fig. 69. The tangent 2-1 is level.

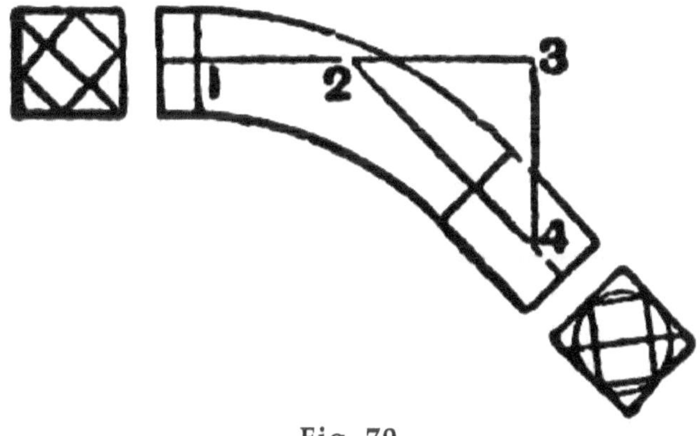

Fig. 70.

To produce the face mould, lay the steel square in the position, indicated by the lines 1, 2, 3, 4, not the figure on the square at the points numbered, and transfer them to a piece of thin stuff, Fig. 70. Line 3-4 in Fig. 70 is indefinite. Now take the length of the long edge of the pitch board in the compasses, and with 2, Fig. 70, as a center, cut the line 3-4 in 4 and draw 2-4. Now 1-2 is the level, and 2-4 is the pitch tangent on the face mold.

To get the bevels and width of the face mold at both ends, take the distance 3-4 on the blade of the square, and the height of a riser on the tongue of the square, apply to the edge of a board and mark by the tongue; this gives the width of the mold at the lower end.

Next take the distance 4-X on the blade of the square, and the distance shown on the pitch board by the line squared from its top edge to the corner, on the tongue of the square; apply to the edge of a board and mark by the tongue; this gives the bevels for the top end of the wreath. Mark the width of the rail on the bevel, and this gives the width of the mold at the top end. An allowance of 6 inches is made at the top end to joint to the straight rail, and two inches at the bottom end to form the miter into the newel cap. The springing line is taken from the pitch board.

Fig. 69, in which are shown the bevels and the pitch board will help to make clear the methods used. The bevel at the back of the pitch board is for the bottom end of the wreath. The triangle has for its base the line 3-4 and for its height one riser. The hypothenuse is the length of 2-4, Fig. 70, and Fig. 70 stands over Fig. 69, level on the line 1-2-3, and inclined from it in this cast at an angle of nearly 45 degrees.

The top end bevel is shown below the pitch board. The angle has for its base the distance 4-x, and for its height not one rise, but the length of a line, from the corner of the pitch board squared from its top edge. This bevel will be understood better by placing the pitch board on the line 2-4 and applying the small triangle to it with its base on the line 4-x, and its point even with the top edge of the pitch board. It will then be at right angles to the top edge of the pitch board.

In practice, a parallel mold is generally used, and the wreath piece is cut out; both thickness of plank and width of molding being equal to the diameter of a circle that will contain a section of finished rail.

Jacques Demoux, Winnipeg, Man., wants to know how to lay out braces, regular and irregular by the use of the Steel Square.

Answer: Braces and trusses are something like rafters and when the run is known, there should be no difficulty in getting the lengths and proper bevels.

In the first place it is always best to make a pattern and then mark out the timber work from the pattern. Suppose we want braces having a "four-foot run"— that is, the brace is to form a diagonal from points four feet from the post and four feet from the girt. Take a piece of stuff already prepared, six feet long, four inches wide and half-inch thick, gauge it three-eighths from jointed edge.

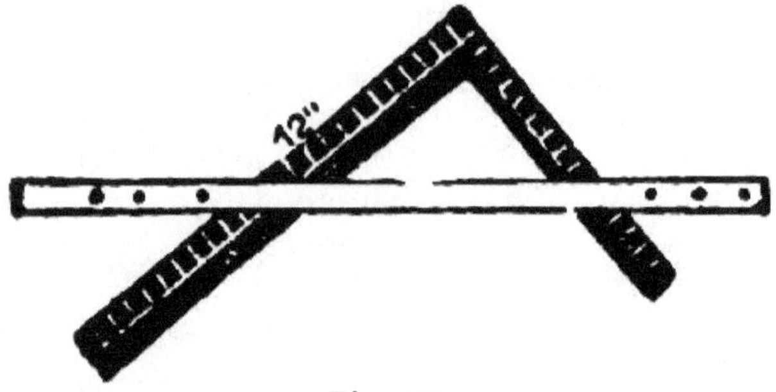

Fig. 71.

Take the square as arranged at Fig. 71, and place it on the prepared stuff as shown at Fig. 72. Adjust the square so that the twelve-inch line coincide exactly with the gauge line o, o, o, o. Hold the square firmly in the position now obtained, and slide the fence up the tongue and blade until it fits snugly against the jointed edge of the prepared stuff, screw the fence tight on the square, and be sure that the 12-inch marks on both the blade and the tongue are in exact position over the gauge-line.

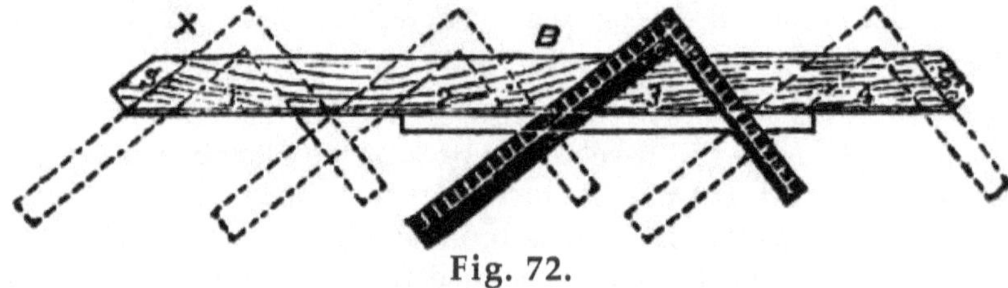

Fig. 72.

We are now ready to lay out the pattern. Slide the square to the extreme left, as shown on the dotted lines at x, mark with a knife on the outside edges of the square, cutting the gauge line. Repeat this process four times, marking the ends, and you have the length and bevels. Square over at each end from the gauge line and you have the toe of the brace. The lines ss, Fig. 72, show the tenons left on the end of the braces.

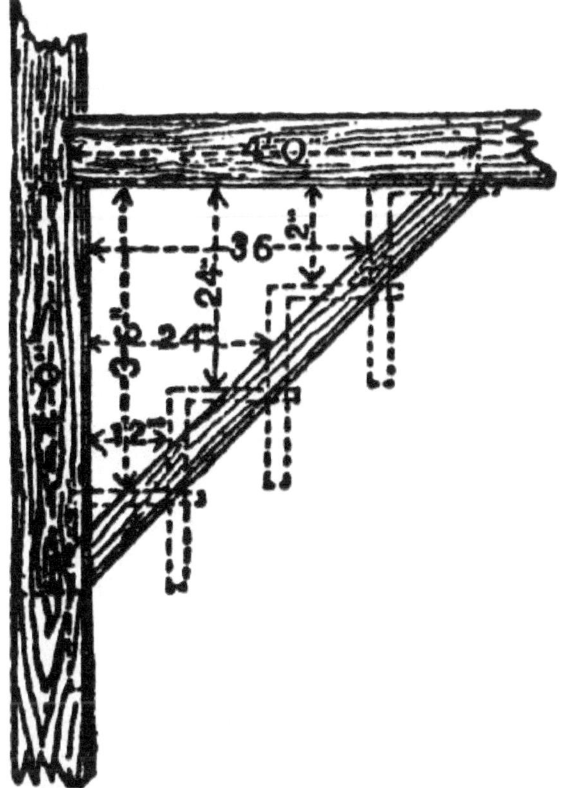

Fig. 73.

The cut at Fig. 73, shows the brace in position, on a reduced scale. The principle on which the square works in the formation of a brace can easily be understood from this cut, as the dotted lines show the position the square was in when the pattern was laid out.

It may be necessary to state that the "square," as now arranged, will lay out a brace pattern for any length, if the angle is right, and the run equal. Should the brace be of great length, however, additional care must be taken in the adjustment of the square, for should there be any departure from truth, that departure will be repeated every time the square is moved, and where it would not affect a short run, it might seriously affect a long one.

To lay out a pattern for a brace where the run on the beam is three feet, and the run down the post four, proceed as follows:

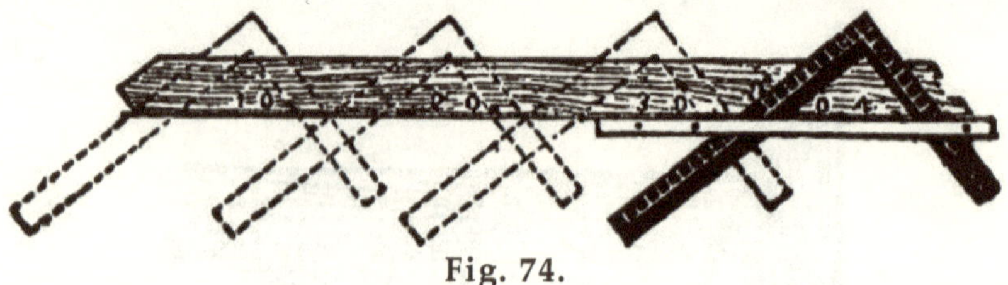

Fig. 74.

Prepare a piece of stuff, same as the one operated on for four feet run; joint and gauge it. Lay the square on the left-hand side, keep the 12-inch mark on the tongue, over the gauge-line; place the 9-inch mark on the blade, on the gauge-line, so that the gauge-line forms the third side of a right angle triangle, the other sides of which are nine and twelve inches, respectively.

Now proceed as on the former occasion, and as shown at Fig. 74, taking care to mark the bevels at the extreme ends. The dotted lines show the position of the square, as the pattern is being laid out.

Fig. 75 shows the brace in position, the dotted lines show where the square was placed on the pattern. It is well to thoroughly understand the method of obtaining the lengths and bevels of irregular braces. A little study will soon enable any person to make all kinds of braces.

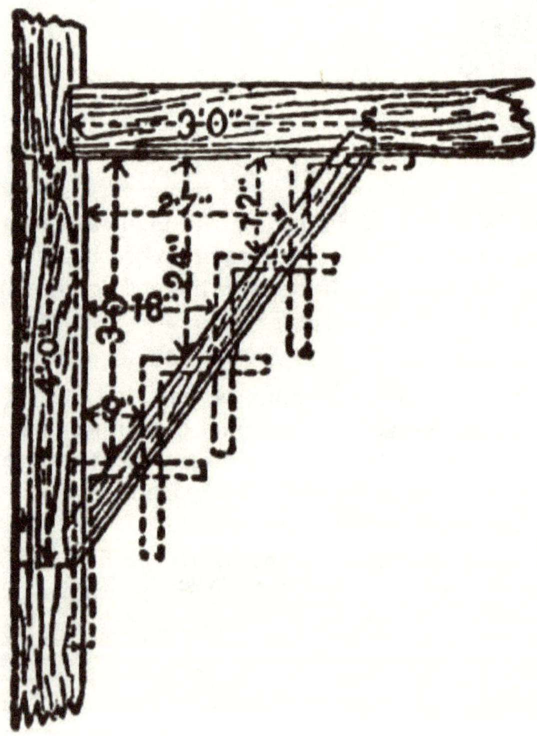

Fig. 75.

If we want a brace with a two-foot run, and a four-foot run it must be evident that, as two is the half of four, so on the square take 12 inches on the tongue, and 6 inches on the blade, apply four times, and we have the length, and the bevels of a brace for this run.

For a three by four foot run, take 12 inches on the tongue and 9 inches on the blade, and apply four times, because, as three feet is ¾ of four feet, so 9 inches is ¾ of 12 inches.

A young carpenter, Toronto, wants to know how to find the center of a circle by aid of the Square.

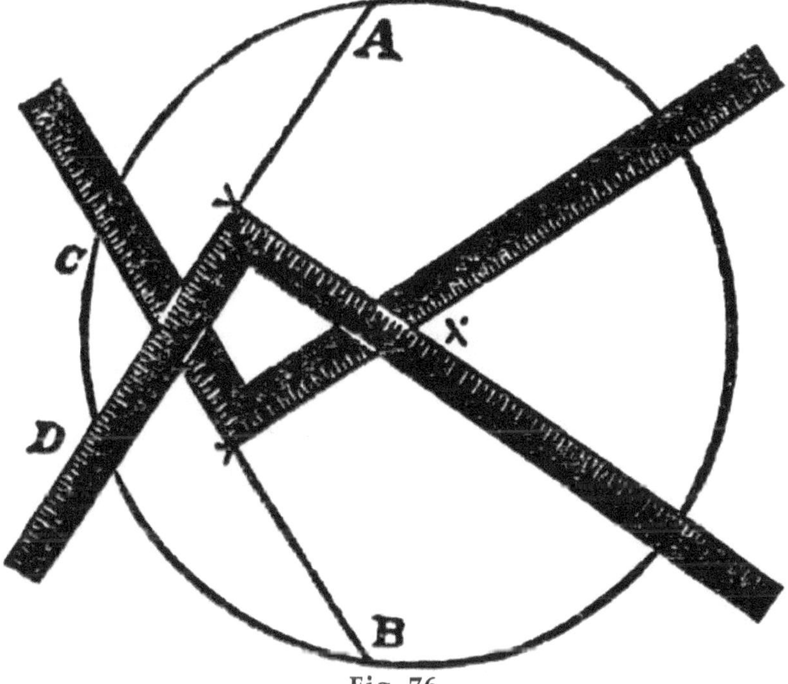

Fig. 76.

Answer: In Fig. 76 is shown how the center of a circle may be determined without the use of compasses; this is based on the principle that a circle can be drawn through any three points that are not actually in a straight line. Suppose we take A, B, C, D for four given points, then draw a line from A to D, and from B to C; get the center of these lines, and square from these centers as shown, and when the square crosses the line, or where the lines intersect, as at x, there will be the center of the circle. This is a very useful rule.

Ed. McDonald, Cincinnati, Ohio, says: "I want to know how much can be done with the square towards setting out stair railing?"

Answer: In a previous page a few remarks on this subject will be found and the following is further submitted:

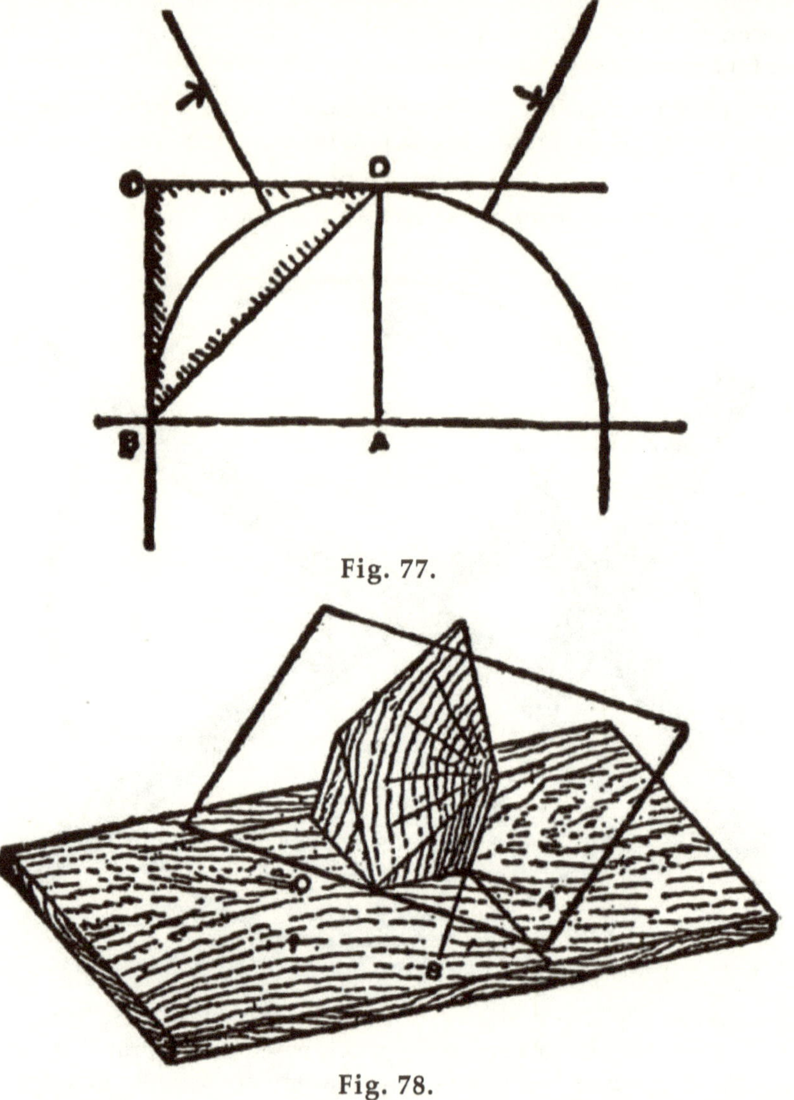

Fig. 77.

Fig. 78.

Fig. 77 shows a plan of a stair well having three winders. The rail in this case will have two different pitches. These rails are a little more complicated than those having equal pitches, as in the latter the major axis is parallel off the diagonal line B D (Fig. 77). When the pitches differ the major axis ceases to be parallel; and the greater the difference in the pitches, the greater will be the difference in the axis and diagonal line. This fact can be easily demonstrated by cutting a model bed block out of 2-inch by 2-inch stuff to equal pitches. Procure a board, and draw a parallel line, say 8 inches off the edge. Now square over a line to cut the first line; set the bed block on, with the back corner touching the intersection of the lines. Lay a piece of cardboard on the inclined face of the bed block, and let it slide down until it touches the board. Make a mark along this edge, and it will be seen, on removing the card, that this line is equidistant from the corner (see Fig. 78). In Fig. 78 the cardboard is shown as though it were transparent. What has just been done is that the plane in which the rail lies has been projected to intersect the horizontal plane which contains the plan of the wreath. The name by which this line is generally known is the horizontal trace (shown at C, Figs. 78 and 79). The minor axis (Figs. 78 and 79) is always parallel off this, and always touches A as in Fig. 77. The major axis (Figs. 78 and 79) also touches this point A, and is always square off the minor axis and off the horizontal trace. It will be seen by this that the rail is pitched equally both ways; therefore the face mold will be of equal width at the ends.

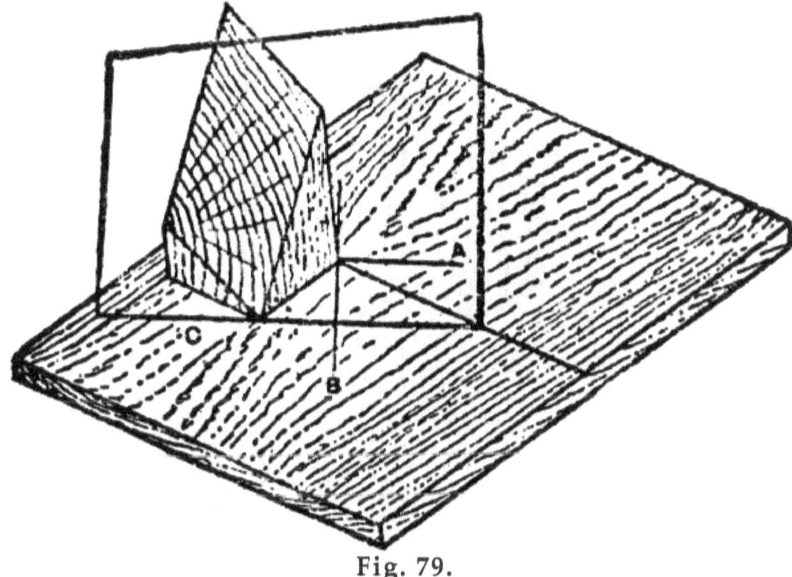

Fig. 79.

When rails are cut by bandsaw on bed blocks, bevels are not necessary, as they can always be obtained by applying a bevel as shown at Fig. 80. The stock should lie solid on the block and square off the sides. When the block is thin it is best to apply the bevel near the corner, when a greater surface is obtained. These bevels are applied after the joint is squared off the tangent lines. To demonstrate a rail with unequal pitches, cut another piece of stuff 2x2 inches, as shown in Fig. 79, repeat the process with the cardboard as before. It will be found that the horizontal trace has departed from the angle of 45 degrees (see Fig. 79) and has approached nearer one corner and gone farther away on the other. The major axis B will have done likewise, as it is always square off the horizontal trace C. The wreath having two pitches, the face mold will obviously be wider at one end than at the other; and if bevels are required, they must be set off on the face of each side of the block. The width of the face mold is to be applied on the tangent line; this makes it slightly in excess on the joint, but it is better to have a little margin in thickness for working. Where thickness of stuff is a secondary consideration, it is preferable to take the rail out of stuff which is as thick as the diameter of a circle that will enclose the section of rail; the corners will then be left complete.

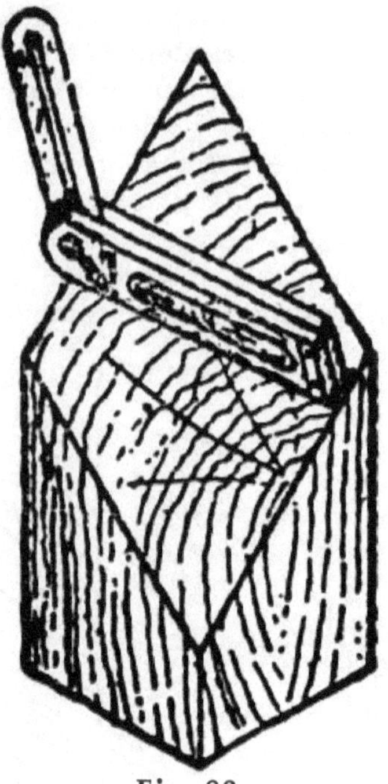

Fig. 80.

The following method shows the least thickness the rail can be cut out of, and also gives width of face molds on the joint. Set the bevel to the bed block as shown at Fig. 80, and apply at the side of the block. Draw a section of rail level; apply the bevel again, touching the bottom corner of the section. The distance between the marks is the thickness, a plumb line marked on shows the width of the face mold on the bevel line. Where the pitches are different the foregoing method has to be applied to each side of the bed block.

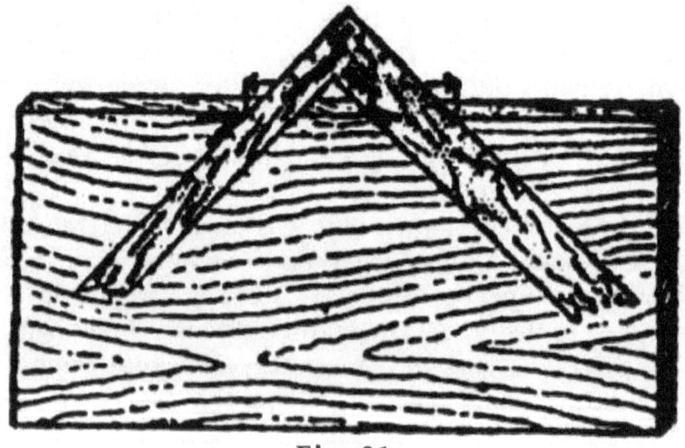

Fig. 81.

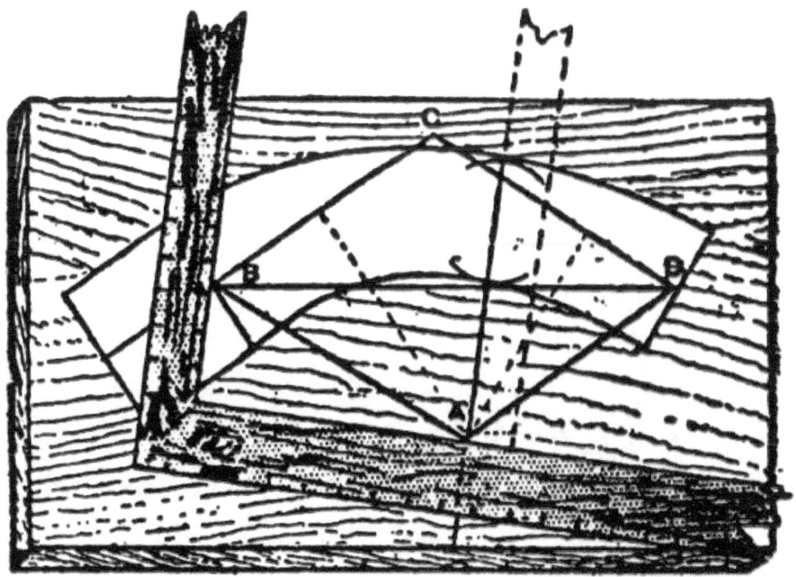

Fig. 82.

The bevels may be also obtained by the steel square. Take the width of prism face (shown by dotted lines) by laying the square with blade on the line C D (Fig. 82) and tongue, cutting at the center A. Note the length on the tongue of the square. Make a mark of this length on the edge of board. Now take the width of A to D (Fig. 84) which is 6 inches off the blade; keep this 6-inch mark fair at the end of this line made on the board (Fig. 81) and push on square until the tongue touches the end of the line; mark by the tongue, and this gives the bevel required.

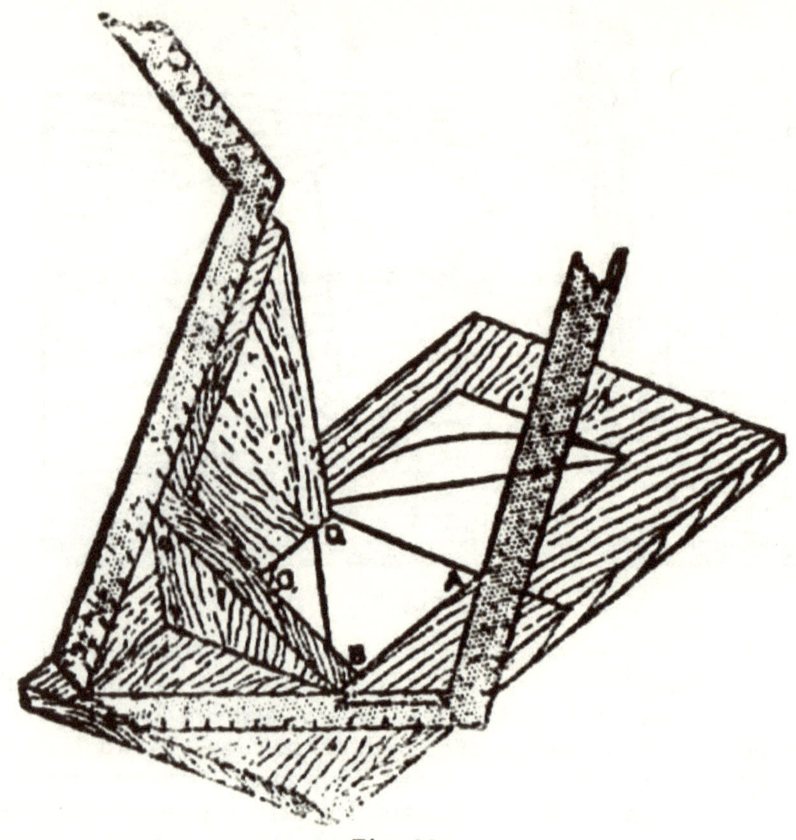

Fig. 83.

To obtain an example of unequal pitches refer to Fig. 84. To set this out, run a line parallel off the edge of the board, and off this line square another. With the intersection A as a center, describe a semi-circle of 6 inches radius. This indicates the center of the rail. Run lines radial from A as shown; these are the riser lines. Draw the lines B C and C D, which are the tangents. Draw the diagonal B D. To make the bed blocks, procure a piece of one inch stuff; take it to the width shown at B C; square on a mark about 3 inches from the end (this is to allow for the shank to clear the saw table; the block is shown at Fig. 83 without the 3-inch allowance). Take on the steel square the rise on tongue and going on blade of the straight flight of stairs; mark on the inch board at tongue; this is pitch of the first tangent. Take the height at D, which is one and a half risers—10½ inches; deduct the height of the first tangent from 10½ inches; take the difference on the tongue and width from C to D on the blade; the tongue gives the cut for the second tangent. Mark the pitch of the first tangent on the edge of the second and cut to this; the pitch of the second tangent gives the edge cut of the first. Cut and fix together with stretcher as previously described.

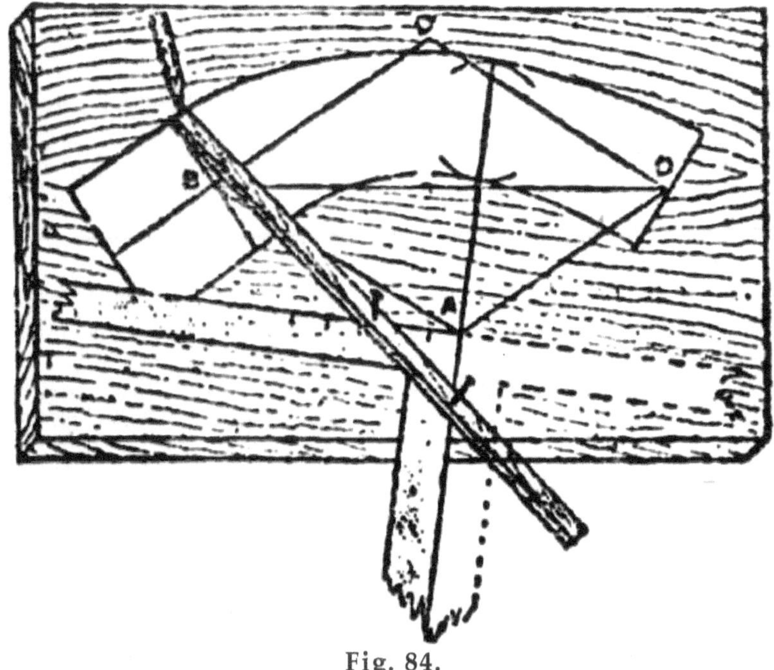

Fig. 84.

To get out the face mold, procure a piece of thin stuff. Three-ply wood is excellent, as though it is liable to warp it does not shrink perceptibly. Shoot on edge and gauge on a center line; take the distance from B to D (Fig. 84) (the hypothenuse of 6 and 6) on the blade and the rise (10½) at D on the tongue; lay on the edge of the board to this. Lay off this length on the three-ply at B D (Fig. 82); take the width B C (Fig. 84) on the blade, rise at C on the tongue; find the hypothenuse, and apply with a pair of compasses at Fig. 82 with B as a center cutting at C. Then apply at D as a center, cutting at A. Now find the hypothenuse C to D (Fig. 84), and apply the compasses as before, with D and B as centers, cutting at A and C. Connect up the points where the arcs intersect to B and D; this is the face of the inclined prism, and contains the true shape of rail. Continue the tangent line C B, 3 inches or whatever is required for the shank, and square the joints of the lines B and D. In order to locate the major axis the horizontal trace is now required. Stand the bed block on the plan (see Fig. 83). Run the blade of the square down until it touches the board; mark this, and remove the block. It will be seen that the bed block has not got the 3 inches allowed at the bottom, but the horizontal trace is as easily found with as without the allowance; all that is required in the former case being to turn the blade to B (still keeping the heel at the top of the bed block), make a mark where the square touches and lay on the square as shown at Fig. 83. Mark at the blade, and slide back the square until the tongue touches at B, and also at the center A. This gives the true horizontal trace and major axis. Note the size indicated by the arrow lines on the tongue (from heel to B). Transfer the square to the three-ply board (Fig. 82), placing it as shown, with the blade touching A, and the distance of the arrow lines at B. Mark along the inside of the blade of the square and slide the square back until the tongue cuts at A. This gives the minor axis. Now continue this line downwards to guide the position of the square shown at Fig. 84. Describe a circle as wide as the rail on the minor axis (Fig. 82). The distance from A (Fig. 84) to the center of the rail is the distance to apply at Fig. 82 for the center of the rail, as this is the point where the center of the rail is fair with the plank. Obtain the width of the face molds, and apply at B and D; lay the square on the major and minor axis as shown at Fig. 84. Lay a lath on the square, with the point touching the outside of the circle at C; drive in a nail at the heel of the square; shift the lath until the point lies at B, and drive in another nail at the side of the square. This trammel is now ready to sweep the outside of the mold, which is done by reversing the square, as shown by dotted lines. Pull out the nails and repeat the process for the inside of the mold.

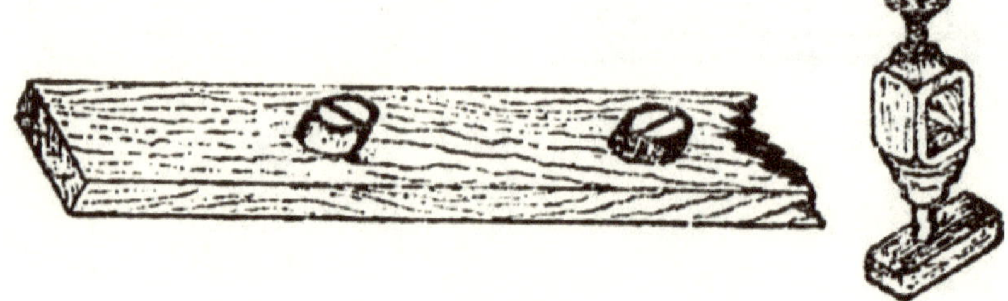

Fig. 85.

Now run parallel lines off the tangent B for the shank; this completes the face mold, which is now ready for the face of the plank. Wreaths for stairs with flights which stand at either acute or obtuse angles to each other may be set out by the methods that have been here described. The only difference, practically, is that the bed block is made acute or obtuse to suit plan of tangents. The device shown at Fig. 85 has been found to answer excellently for striking out ellipses. To make this, procure two screws

¾ inches long, also a piece of brass tube that will just slip on the plain part of the screw without shaking. Counter sink out the ends until the screw heads are flush; cut two pieces off the tube three- sixteenths and file up true—these pieces are best held by sinking them with a bit in a piece of hardwood. Now when about to strike an ellipse, drive these screws in with the collars on to half major and minor, measured from the point of the trammel to the inside of the collar for the major, and to the outside of the collar for the minor. It will be found that if the collar has been made true, the trammel will slip around the curve without causing the square to slip about, the collars acting as rollers.

T. Jones, Boise City, Idaho, would like to know of a ready way to frame hip roofs and roofs of irregular or different pitches with the steel square, including lengths and bevels of all rafters.

Answer: These problems along with many others are discussed and explained at length in my larger works on the Steel Square, but the following, which is somewhat condensed, does to some extent cover Mr. Jones' inquiries:

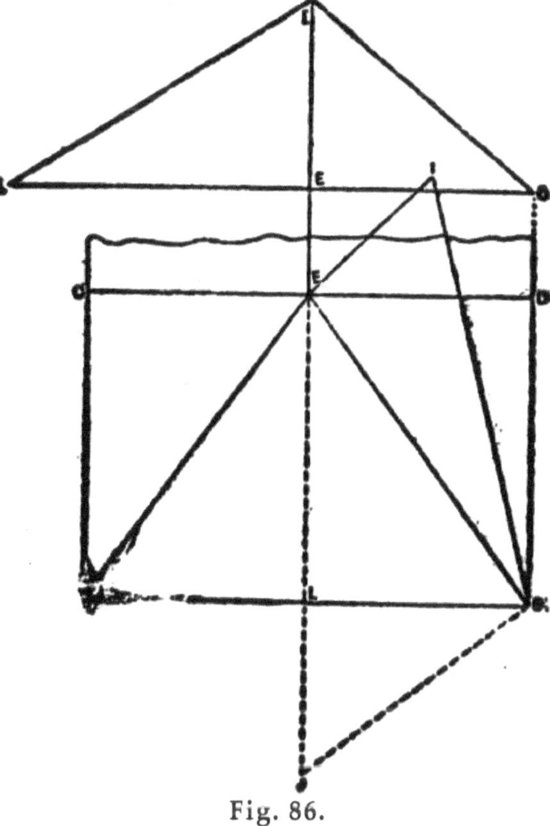

Fig. 86.

Suppose A, B, C, D, Fig. 86, to represent one end of a hip roof with a span of 24 feet and a 10-foot rise. The side rafter I D shown in top sketch will have a run of 12 feet. The common rafter at the end of building, I L, has a run of 16 feet, with the same rise, so that the ends and sides of the roofs have different pitches. The lengths and cuts of the common rafters are obtained as shown in Fig. 87, by taking 12 on the blade and 10 on the tongue of the square and measuring across, giving the length of the side rafter, from which one-half the thickness of the ridge, measured square back from the plumb cut, must be deducted. The blade gives the foot cut and the tongue the plumb cut. The length of the end rafter is obtained by taking 16 on the blade and 10 on the tongue, which will of course give the respective cuts also. The same results may be obtained by applying the square to a straight edge and marking along the blade and tongue, which will give a gauge line to which a bevel may be set. By taking 16 on the blade and 12 on the tongue, as shown in Fig. 90, the run of the hip rafters, 20, is obtained.

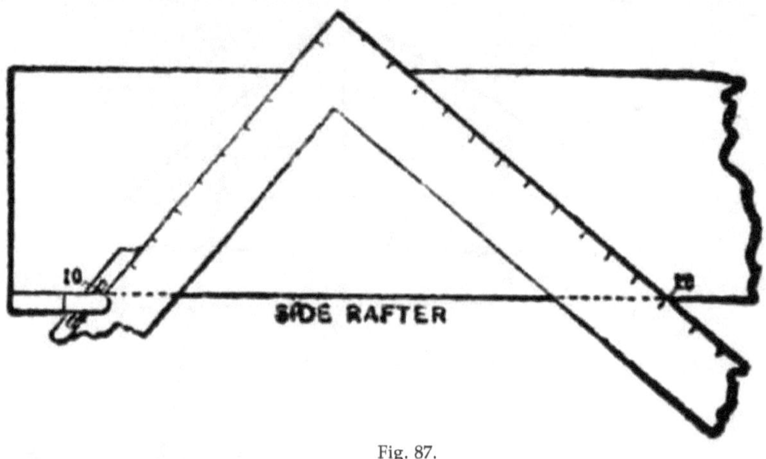

Fig. 87.

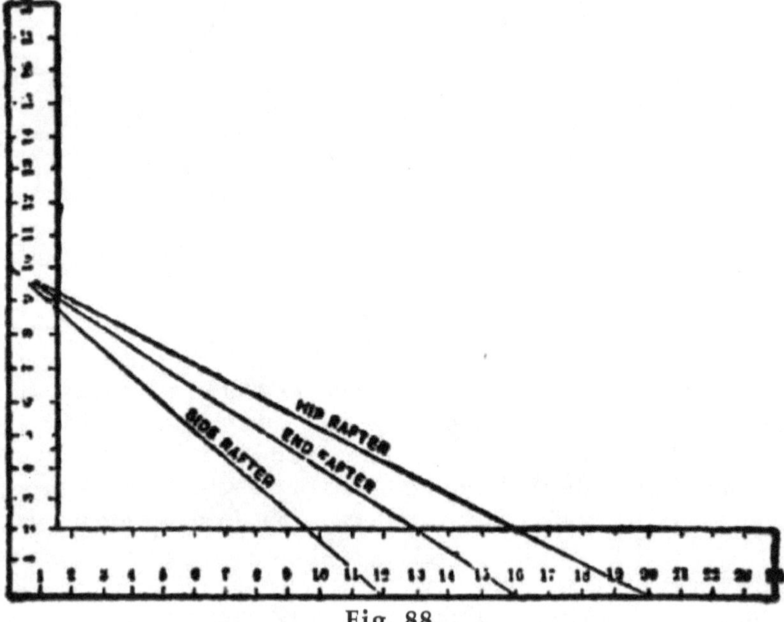

Fig. 88.

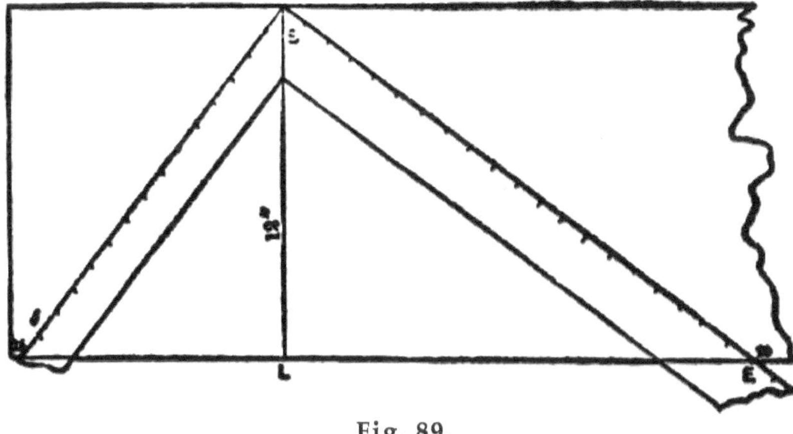

Fig. 89.

Referring to Fig. 88, it will be seen that 20 on the blade and 10 on the tongue give the seat and plumb cuts of the hip together with the length, after one-half the thickness of the ridge has been deducted from the side cut. The side cut is found in a slightly different way from that of a regular hip or valley on an ordinary roof. The common method is to take the length of the hip on the blade and run on the tongue, but this will not work in this case, as the run of the hip does not be at an angle of 45 degrees as in ordinary roofs. The line B J in Fig. 86 must first be obtained, as shown in Fig. 89. Joint one edge of a board and square up the line B L. Measure one-half the width of building—in inches—on this line, 12 in this case, and with the heel of the square at the point B, move the square until 20 on the blade touches the edge of the board at E. The tongue will then give the point J 15 inches; which is the length of the line required.

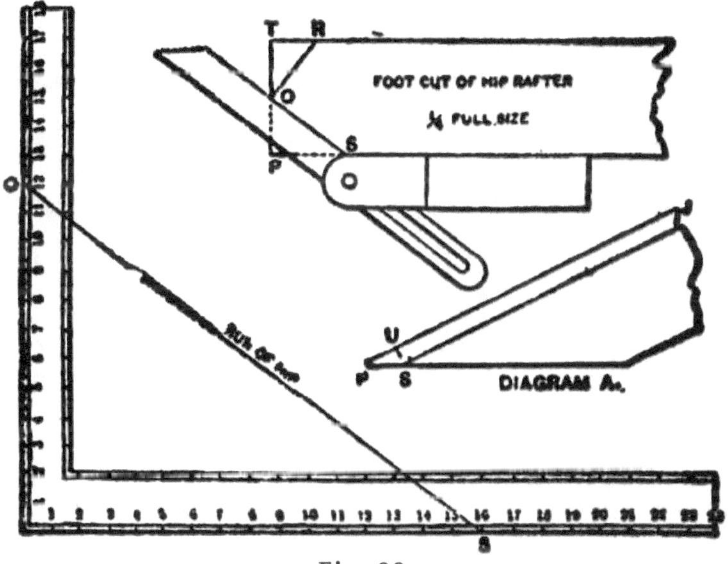

Fig. 90.

Then take this line on the tongue and the length of the hip on the blade, Fig. 90, and the blade will give the bevel of the hip to lie against the ridge. As a general rule, hip rafters are not backed, but if such is desired the lines for backing can be found by setting it to the foot cut of the hip rafter. Make O R square with S O and gauge back as shown in the diagram A. Do the same on the other side, using the distance T R instead of P S. The point O is of course at the center of the line T P.

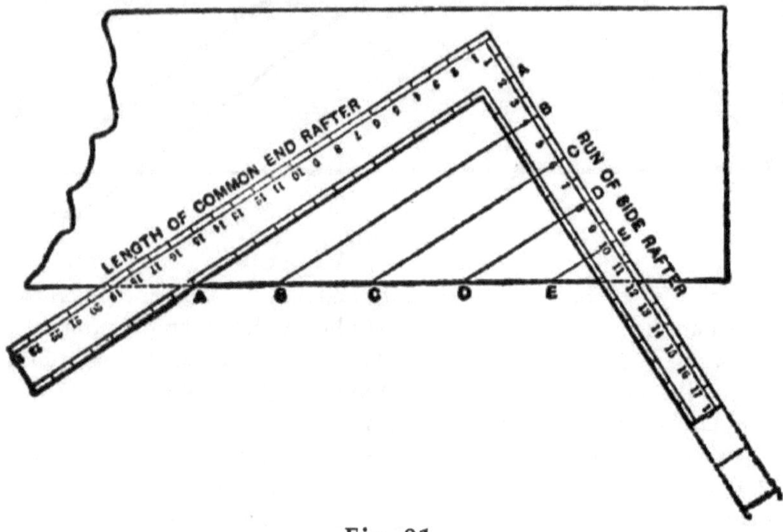

Fig. 91.

For lengths and bevels of jacks, proceed as follows: For end of roof, and set 2 feet on centers, take a board and apply the square to it, as shown in Fig. 91, with the length of the end rafter on the blade and the run of the side rafter on the tongue. Space off 2, 4, 6, 8 and 10 in. on the tongue after marking along both blade and tongue. The lines, AA, BB, CC, DD, EE, will give the length of the jacks, as well as the side cut to fit the side of the hip, the square being moved down along tongue line, while the run of the end rafter on blade and its rise on tongue will give the seat and plumb cuts. For the side jacks, Fig. 92 gives the same method, only that the length of the side rafter is taken on the blade and the run of the end rafter on the tongue. If it is so desired, the length of the jack rafter $A^1 A^1$ may be deducted from the length of the common rafter, which will give the difference in the lengths of the jacks.

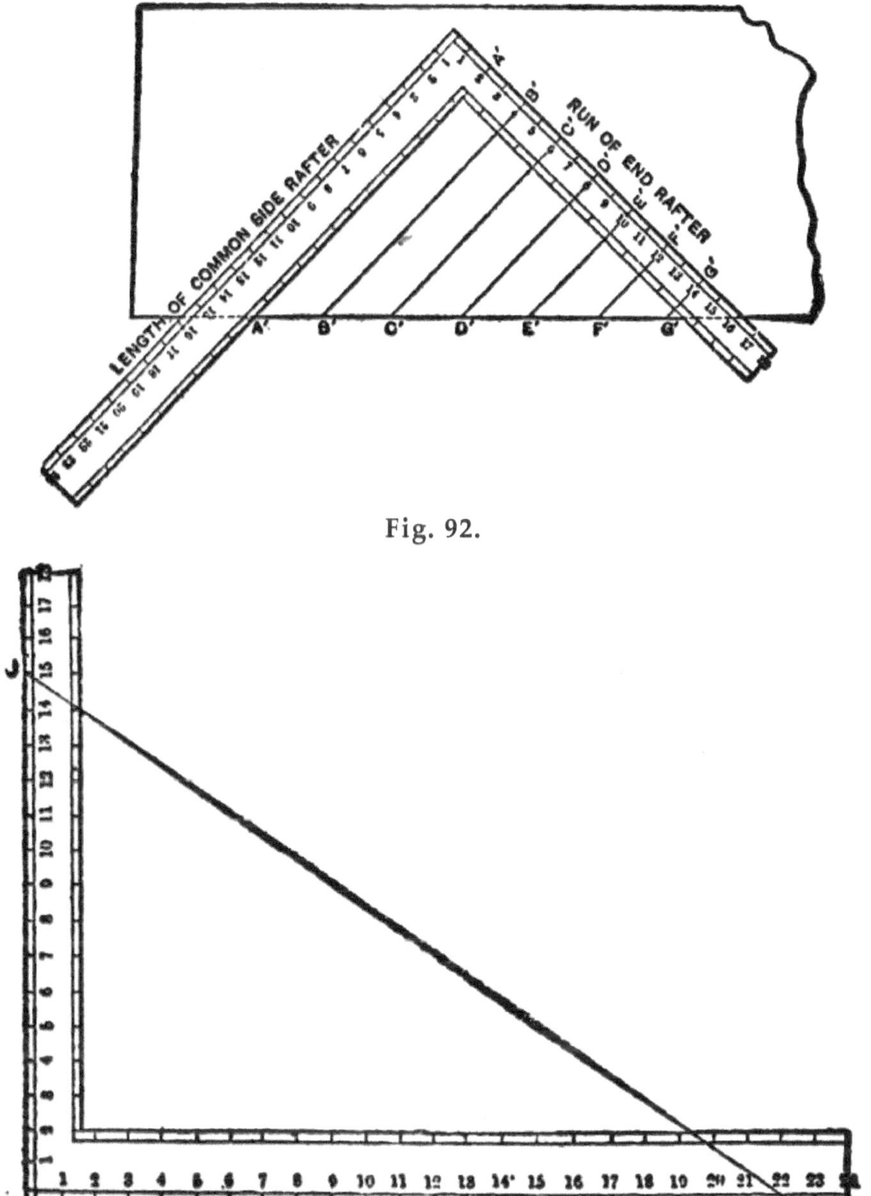

Fig. 92.

Fig. 93.

The rules and diagrams, given herewith will apply to valley as well as hip rafters, and may be relied upon as being accurate if closely followed.

RULE—See Fig. 87.

Tongue.	Blade.
12″	16″ gives run of hip.
10″	12″ gives length of side rafter.
10″	16″ gives length of end rafter.
10″	20″ gives length of hip rafter.

RULE—See Fig. 91.

Blade.				Tongue.
Common End Rafter	19″			12′
Longest Jack		15	10/12″	10′
4th " "		12	8/12″	8′
3d " "		9	6/12″	6′
2d " "		6	4/12″	4′
Shortest " "		3	2/12″	2′

Blade gives Side Cut of Jacks.

RULE—See Fig. 92.

Blade.		Tongue.'
Common Side Rafter	15′ 7½″	16′
Longest Jack "	13′ 8″	14′
6th " "	11′ 8½″	12′
5th " "	9′ 9″	10′
4th " "	7′ 9½″	8′
3d " "	5′ 10″	6′
2d " "	3′ 10½″	4′
1st " "	1′ 11″	2′

Blade gives Cut of Jacks, also Sheathing.

Blade gives Cut of Jacks, also Sheathing.

These matters have been discussed at length, in trade journals and also in my larger volumes on The Practical Uses of the Steel Square, but the foregoing treatment of the subject is on somewhat different lines and will prove interesting.

John Wilberforce, Toronto, Ont., wants to know if a wreath piece for a single-pitch rail with level landing can be set out with the Steel Square.

Answer: Yes, the problem can be solved as follows:

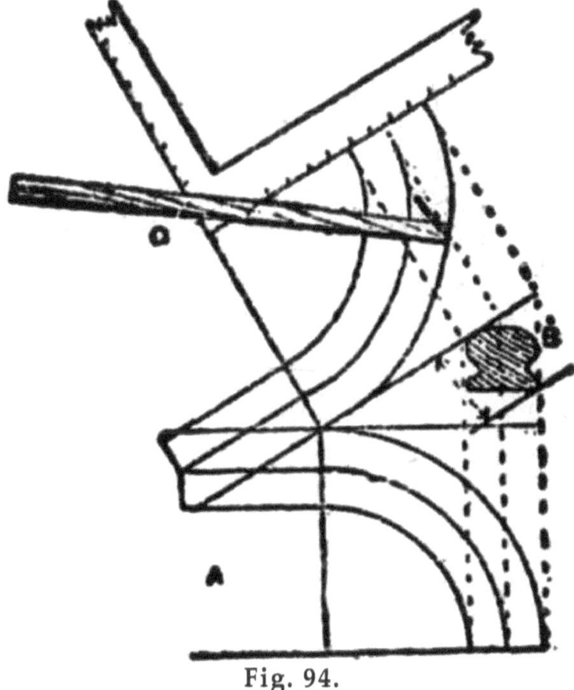

Fig. 94.

Set out on a board the plan of the wreath A (Fig. 94). Draw the outside circle and the inside and center line of same, showing also the joints. Set out the pitch off the shank; square up the center outside and inside lines from the plan on to the pitch. The thickness of the wreath piece is found by drawing a section of rail under the pitch line B. Set out again the half-width of the well; square off the pitch lines to the half width; this gives major and minor axes of the ellipse, as shown in the development (Fig. 94). Lay the square on the axis. Get a light piece of lath, drive in a nail at the half major, and one at the half minor; describe the inner ellipse line on the piece of timber from which the wreath is to be formed; pull out the nails, and repeat the process for the center and outside lines. Draw the shank and also the point as shown on the board.

Fig. 95.

Now cut at the joints, allowing an ⅛-inch for the fitting of the joint after the wreath is cut and roughed out. Use another piece of timber about 2 inches thick, to form the bed block, and cut it to the pitch accurate and square in thickness. Screw or pin it to the under side of the wreath piece (see Fig. 95), taking care to get it parallel with the shank, and the nails in clear of the saw. Then proceed to cut the wreath with the band saw, beginning at the circular part, and work it to the shank inside and outside. This operation should be performed most carefully with a narrow band saw, having a strong set and strained tight, feeding very slowly. The wreath should require hardly any spoke shaving. Knock off the block and draw a chalk mark across the table, just in front of the teeth. The use of this line is to assist the operator to get the outside of the wreath always touching this spot in front of the saw. He must carefully lower his hand until it is down level at the shank end. The top is cut first, and the saw should skim along the outside top arris, giving a sweep that cannot be excelled in graduation of curve. Then set a gauge to the thickness of the rail, mark a line on the inside of the wreath, and cut as before. With a little practice a wreath can be turned off the band saw ready for molding. When the shank is too long, it is always better to nail the bed block on top of the wreath, and cut it upside down, thus getting the curve portion near the table. Then the shank can be run in with the band saw when the block is knocked off. The foregoing is for a single-pitch wreath as used for stairs with level landings and narrow wells. Where the rails are pitched both ways, the bed block has to be cut at the double inclination. (See preceding answers.)

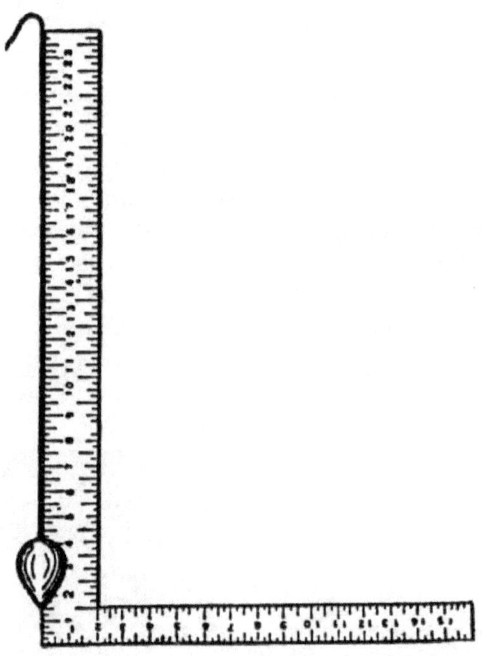

Lector House believes that a society develops through a two-fold approach of continuous learning and adaptation, which is derived from the study of classic literary works spread across the historic timeline of literature records. Therefore, we aim at reviving, repairing and redeveloping all those inaccessible or damaged but historically as well as culturally important literature across subjects so that the future generations may have an opportunity to study and learn from past works to embark upon a journey of creating a better future.

This book is a result of an effort made by Lector House towards making a contribution to the preservation and repair of original ancient works which might hold historical significance to the approach of continuous learning across subjects.

HAPPY READING & LEARNING!

LECTOR HOUSE LLP
E-MAIL: lectorpublishing@gmail.com